El Salvador
A War by Proxy

by

Keith Preston

El Salvador
A War by Proxy
by
Keith Preston

ISBN-13: 978-1-908476-31-9

Black House Publishing Ltd
Kemp House
152 City Road
London
UNITED KINGDOM
EC1V 2NX

www.blackhousepublishing.co.uk
Email: info@blackhousepublishing.co.uk

Contents

Contents

El Salvador
A War by Proxy

For the people of El Salvador

Introduction

The Central American nation of El Salvador was consumed by a bloody civil war between 1980 and 1992. The principal players in the conflict were the right-wing government of El Salvador, a coalition of rebel groups operating under the umbrella of the Farabundo Marti National Liberation Front, and the Reagan administration in the United States. The U.S. supported the Salvadoran government. During the course of the war, in a nation whose population numbered slightly more than five million, an estimated 75,000 people were killed; 18,000 disappeared. Over a million fled the country into exile, and another million were left homeless.[1]

The precise amount of financial aid provided by the United States to the Salvadoran regime during the war has never been determined, but the most common and credible estimates range between six and seven billion dollars. In addition, the United States provided training to members of the Salvadoran armed forces, not only within El Salvador itself, but also in Honduras, the Panama Canal Zone, and in the United States. Military aid to the Salvadoran regime was also provided by the US through Israel, and by other Latin America nations partially as a result of American pressure. The Salvadoran armed forces also received sophisticated aircraft from the United States. These were used in the prosecution of the war. While American military personnel never officially participated in the war effort itself, US military advisors and intelligence personnel were assigned to El Salvador for the duration of the war and are widely believed to have participated in actual combat activities on an informal and frequently clandestine basis. Private mercenaries from the United States are also known to have fought in the Salvadoran civil war.[2]

The civil war began during the twilight of the Carter administration, which provided support to the right-wing government against whom the rebels took up arms. It was during the presidency of Ronald Reagan and his successor, George H.W. Bush, that most of the war took place. The years between 1980, when the initial show of support to the Salvadoran regime by the Carter administration evolved into the harder line taken by the incoming Reagan government, and 1983, when the policies that would guide the conduct of the American government for the duration of the war were already well-established, are crucial. It was during these years that the essence of American foreign policy towards El Salvador was formed. This work will examine the relationship between the foreign policy of the United States and the civil war in El Salvador on several levels.

First, the relationship of El Salvador with the United States and the role of this relationship as a component part of the wider U.S. client-state system in Latin America will be discussed. Second, the significance of El Salvador, a tiny nation with no international influence, to the broader paradigm of American foreign policy elites generally and the Reagan administration specifically will be studied. Lastly, a special focus will be given to the early years of the Salvadoran civil war between 1980 and 1983, covering the final phase of the Carter administration policy, and the policies of the early years of the Reagan administration. It was during these years that the essential foundations for the conduct of U.S. foreign policy during the course of the war were firmly established.

This work will examine US foreign policy towards El Salvador from the perspective of inquiry into possible answers to five primary questions. The first of these questions will examine the Salvadoran civil war as it developed out of the historic class relationships of Salvadoran society, out of the international relationship between El Salvador and the United States, and out of traditional United States foreign policy concerning Latin America. It will be shown that the civil war was the natural outgrowth of these relationships with its roots in the original expropriation of the indigenous inhabitants and peasant classes of El Salvador, the subsequent development of

North/South relations in the Western Hemisphere on the client-state system model, and the subordination of the Salvadoran nation to the hegemony of American foreign policy objectives in Latin America. The failure of both the Salvadoran elite and the United States to seriously address the persistent exploitation of the impoverished classes of El Salvador helped to create a situation where civil war became inevitable.

The second question will examine how the Salvadoran civil war began during the latter period of the Jimmy Carter administration. During Carter's final days in office, he ordered an aid package to El Salvador that included ten million U.S. dollars in financial assistance along with the support of American military advisors.[3] The role of the Carter administration in financing and propping up the Salvadoran junta, while knowing perfectly well the nature of that regime, and thereby making a lengthy and protracted civil war all but inevitable, will be examined as a crucial moment in American-Salvadoran relations and one that set the stage for what transpired during the Reagan years.

The third major question to be examined in this work will involve a discussion of the intersection between the escalation of the Salvadoran civil war as it was unfolding in the early 1980s and the coming to power of the Reagan government during the same period. With regards to the Salvadoran civil war, it will be shown that the war was one that essentially pitted the Salvadoran state, ruling oligarchy and military against not only insurgent armed rebel forces but also against the wider civilian population of El Salvador, particularly the peasant classes, and, indeed, against civil society itself. It will be shown that the policy of the Reagan administration was to pursue narrowly-focused geopolitical objectives, wrapped in the banner of ideological extremism, and without regard for the human costs or regional consequences of such a policy. The atrocities committed by the Salvadoran armed forces and private paramilitary and vigilante groups (massacres, torture, repression, etc.) during the early 1980s were widely known and widely documented during that time. Reagan administration officials not only had full knowledge of these events as they were transpiring, but also played a major role in obscuring such incidents, and lying to the U.S. Congress, media, public, etc. about such occurrences. This was the norm with the Reagan administration from the onset of President Reagan's coming to power. Such an approach was well-established during Reagan's first few years in office and became the norm for the rest of his tenure as president as well as that of President George H. W. Bush. [4]

The fourth question will examine the Salvadoran opposition. It will be shown that the FMLN insurgency evolved out of earlier attempts at armed struggle waged by disparate radical groups, and was made possible only when the heavy-handedness of the Salvadoran ruling class pushed virtually the entire array of dissident opinion in El Salvador towards a formal military alliance for the purpose of overthrowing the state. The armed resistance was rooted in the desperate political and economic conditions in El Salvador, and not in pressure from external forces such as Nicaragua, Cuba or the Soviet Union as U.S. policy makers claimed. The opposition was not motivated by a commitment to hard-line Marxist-Leninist ideology, as the Reagan administration consistently suggested, but rather by a newer kind of radicalism with its roots in the progressive wing of the Catholic Church of Latin America. The revolutionary movement in El Salvador, like its counterparts in some other Latin American countries during the same period, was a departure from the more orthodox Marxist-Leninist, pro-Soviet or Maoist ideological foundation common to other Third World "national liberation" struggles of the latter part of the twentieth century. Special focus will be given to the role of dissidents within the Church in the development of resistance movements in Latin America generally and El Salvador specifically. Without the role of the Church, the Salvadoran resistance would never have developed in the form that it did, and perhaps it would not have developed to nearly as significant a level as it did at all.

The final question will address the overall impact of Reagan administration policy with regards to the Salvadoran civil war. It is known that the U.S. provided substantial aid and limited numbers of military advisers to the Salvadoran government, but the role of American officials in shaping the actual prosecution of the Salvadoran government's war effort against the rebel forces, and of American assistance in keeping the Salvadoran regime in power, was much more extensive than what is widely understood. The American policy makers largely directed the war itself, and the Salvadorans were comparable to mercenaries acting on behalf of the Reagan administration. The real war was between the U.S. and the FMLN rebel forces. The Salvadoran state was more a proxy force. El Salvador's then-President Jose Napoleon Duarte admitted as much in a 1984 interview when he said:

> The root of this problem is such that the aid is given under such conditions that its use is really decided by the Americans and not by us. Decisions like how many planes or helicopters we buy, how we spend our money, how many trucks we need, how many bullets and of what caliber, how many pairs of boots and where our priorities should be — all of that...And all of the money is spent over there. We never even see a penny of it, because everything arrives already paid for.[5]

This is not to say that the Salvadoran state and oligarchy did not have its own interests to maintain and did not desire its own survival. Yet the escalation of the war as well as the particular character of the war effort was shaped by the pressures placed on the Salvadoran regime by the Americans, the Christian Democratic-Salvadoran military ruling coalition and the election of Duarte to the presidency being foremost among these.

No assessment of U.S. foreign policy in Central America during the period of the Salvadoran civil war would be complete without an examination of the justifying rationales used by the

American policy makers. Foremost among these, of course, were the Reagan government's professed concerns about alleged Soviet and Cuban influence in the Central American nations. These issues constituted the primary rationale for the policies provided by U.S. foreign policy officials to the U.S. public. The policy makers typically justified their positions and actions by appealing to strategic geopolitical considerations pertaining to the Cold War rivalry with the Soviet Union along with the ideology of anti-communism. This rationale will be critiqued, utilizing both primary and secondary sources, and compared with alternate explanations for the motivations and objectives of US policy makers. The rhetoric of policy makers and US officials will be compared with available historical facts concerning the Salvadoran civil war as a means of determining the truthfulness of the claims of these officials.

The conventional narrative maintains that the American government was concerned primarily with avoiding yet another leftist revolution in Latin America such as those that had previously occurred in Cuba in 1959 and Nicaragua in 1979. Preventing such a revolution was important to the Americans so as to avoid the establishment of Cuban-model Soviet "beachheads" (client states and/or military outposts) in Latin America. American foreign policy elites purportedly feared that the recent Nicaraguan Revolution would have the effect of establishing that nation as a "second Cuba," i.e., a Communist ally of the Soviet Union in Latin America, and that the Nicaraguans, with the assistance of the Cubans and the Soviets, were "exporting their revolution" to the other nations of Central America, such as Honduras, Guatemala, or El Salvador. Presumably, the eventual Communist and/or pro-Soviet conquest of the nations of Central America would lead to the spread of "communism," or anti-American leftist revolutions, to still more Latin American or Caribbean nations including the US border state of Mexico. At that point, so this line of geopolitical reasoning went, the nations on the southern border of the United States would have been brought into the "orbit" of America's archrival, the Soviet

Union, perhaps even incorporated into the Soviet-led Warsaw Pact. The United States would be increasingly surrounded by a "sea of red."[6] President Reagan summarized his administration's position in a March 14, 1983 address to the American public:

> If Central America were to fall, what would the consequences be for our position in Asia and Europe and for our alliances such as NATO: If the U.S. cannot respond to threats near our border, why should the Europeans or Asians believe we are seriously concerned about threats to them? If the Soviets can assume that nothing short of an actual attack on the U.S. will provoke an American response, which ally, which friend will trust us then? [7]

Critics of the Reagan administration's rhetoric regarding Central America ranged from moderates, who considered such claims to be exaggerated, to much harsher critics who denounced the administration's positions as paranoid and hysterical, perhaps even insane. [8] The Reagan government's policy of staunch support for the established right-wing governments of El Salvador, Guatemala and Honduras as well as the *"contra"* rebel groups attempting to overthrow the left-wing government of Nicaragua was extremely controversial within domestic U.S. society, international opinion, and the American government itself. To many Americans, the sending of U.S. military advisors to El Salvador in the early 1980s was frighteningly reminiscent of the early stages of America's disastrous involvement in Vietnam twenty years earlier. Despite President Reagan's landslide victories in the 1980 and 1984 elections, public opinion polls consistently indicated that his administration's Central America policy was unpopular among the American public. The administration also faced strong opposition from influential members of the U.S. Congress over the question of Central America.

Congressional critics, U.S. antiwar activists and many leading voices of international opinion alike considered the

Reagan government's policies to be flagrant in their disregard for humanitarian concerns and questions of social justice in the region. In 1969, future President of El Salvador Napoleon Duarte had said that the purpose of U.S. foreign policy in Latin America was to "maintain the Iberoamerican countries in a condition of direct dependence on the international political decisions most beneficial to the United States, both at the hemisphere and the world levels. (The Americans) preach to us of democracy while everywhere they support dictatorships." Does this available evidence support Duarte's contention? That is a question this thesis will attempt to answer.[9]

Most existing scholarship concerning the relationship between the Salvadoran civil war and American foreign policy during the same period approaches the issues from one of three perspectives. The first is an approach that might be described as "America-centric." This methodology treats domestic issues within El Salvador as side issues, and often implicitly regards their significance or relevance as dependent upon their relationship to U.S. foreign policy objectives, or their relationship to the wider Cold War conflict between the United States and the Soviet Union. A particularly egregious example of this approach is *Strategies of Containment*, a work by John Lewis Gaddis on the history of the Cold War. Gaddis' review of the Reagan era *does not include a single reference to El Salvador*. This is rather extraordinary, given that Reagan administration officials claimed the wars in Central America were vital to American security interests and the prevention of the establishment of Soviet influence in the Western hemisphere.

Certainly, one might be inclined to think that tens of thousands of deaths, a million refugees and billions of dollars spent by the American government are significant enough to merit mention in a general history of U.S. foreign policy during the Cold War.[10]

A second approach might be characterized as "idealist."

Such an approach will evaluate American policy in places such as El Salvador with a primary focus on the impact of U.S. foreign policy on human rights concerns, the advancement of "democracy," international peace and other such concerns. A work of this type is Gaddis Smith's *Morality, Reason and Power*, an overview of the Carter administration's foreign policy, including human rights issues raised by Carter. The following statement by Smith summarizes the presumptions behind his work fairly well:

> American foreign policy-indeed, the foreign policy of any democratic state, must always pursue three broad objectives: security against the military power of present or potential enemies: the economic well-being of the population; and the preservation of democratic values... Jimmy Carter entered office believing that the failure of his predecessors was moral. He promised a government and especially a foreign policy "as good as the people"... Carter failed because he asked the American people to think as citizens of the world with an obligation toward future generation. He offered a morally responsible and farsighted vision. But the clamor of political critics, the behavior of the Soviet Union, the discordant voices of his advisers, and the impossibility of seeing clearly what needed to be done, all combined to make Carter's vision appear naïve.[11]

Such an approach will typically characterize American foreign policy concerning nations such as El Salvador as misguided, though perhaps well-intentioned, with errors or failures being the result of either the ordinary human flaws of policy makers, impossible situations brought on by un-chosen circumstances, or the "failure of America to live up to its ideals."

A third approach is the kind usually associated with writers or commentators of the "far left," for example, Noam Chomsky, Howard Zinn, William Blum, Peter Dale Scott, Alexander

Cockburn or Michael Parenti.[12] Such an approach might be characterized as "moralist," meaning that American foreign policy is criticized within the context of perceived moral failures of policy makers, and the villainous opposition of U.S. foreign policy elites to human rights, social justice, peace and other such high-minded values.

This book attempts a kind of synthesis of all of these approaches, yet attempts to tell the story from the "bottom up." While this is a work on U.S. foreign policy, a conscious effort is made to tell the story from the perspective of those most negatively impacted by that set of policies. The Cold War context in which American foreign policy with regards to the Salvadoran civil war was formed is recognized, yet much of the Cold War rationale for these policies is assailed. The supposed "idealism" of American foreign policy, including that of the Carter administration, is approached with skepticism, yet genuine accomplishments in areas such as human rights improvements are not ignored. While, in the author's view, American foreign policy in El Salvador during the 1980s merits the criticism that Chomsky, Zinn, et. al. have heaped upon it, the author is less interested in moral condemnation of U.S. policy makers than in simply interpreting a Hobbesian world of brawling nations from the perspective of one of the "little guys." In some ways, the implications of the conclusions of this study are "conservative" in nature. The disastrous effects of U.S. hegemony in El Salvador are shown to be a likely and predictable consequence of empire-building and imperial expansionism. The failure of Carter's human rights policies raises questions as to whether American power can genuinely be a force for the advancement of idealist objectives (such as "democracy and human rights") in other parts of the world, or whether such influence is actually an obstacle to progress elsewhere. Also, the grotesque nature of Reagan administration policy in El Salvador provides illustration of the excesses associated with the administration's ideological extremism and fanaticism.

Two terms that will appear repeatedly in this work are

"client state" and "proxy war." Therefore, these terms merit the provision of a working definition from the outset.

For purposes of this book, a "client state" is used to describe states that function as *de facto* puppets or vassalages to the United States, within the framework of American imperial hegemony. These states are not literal colonies, but operate as part of a system whereby local elites are subject to favoritism and preferential treatment on the part of U.S. policy makers, and provided with protection from internal revolution, in exchange for the subordination of these elites' own peoples' national, cultural or economic interests to the interests of the American ruling class. A "proxy war" is a process by which the United States wages war against forces resisting imperial domination, whether these are states seeking national independence, such as Nicaragua during this period, or movements carrying out a revolution against local elites who operate as clients of U.S. imperialism, such as the resistance forces in El Salvador. In a "proxy war," the actual war effort is not carried out primarily by the armed forces of the United States, but by local forces armed and funded by the United States, such as the *contra* forces of Nicaragua, or the Salvadoran state.

Comments on Primary Sources

One of the provisions of the 1992 Peace Accords that signified the end of the Salvadoran civil war was the creation of a United Nations Commission on the Truth, whose purpose was to investigate human rights abuses in El Salvador during the course of the war. The Commission released its report in March, 1993.

Among its findings was that the American government had allowed Salvadoran exiles operating in Miami to direct terrorist activities in El Salvador from within the territory of the United States. Some members of the U.S. Congress were disturbed by this finding and asked for the declassification of various CIA, State Department, and Defense Department documents pertaining to El Salvador. The Clinton administration complied with this request, releasing more than 12,000 such documents. These documents are now available for public examination through the National Security Archives, a non-governmental organization whose reading room is located at George Washington University in Washington, D.C and whose files are available to university libraries on a subscription basis. This is a collection of documents available on micofiche detailing U.S. foreign policy in the years prior to the onset of the Salvadoran civil war and the early years of the war during the first term of the Reagan administration.[13]

The United Nations' *Report of the Commission on the Truth for El Salvador* is also publicly available, as are numerous other documents produced by the U.S. foreign policy establishment during the war. One of these is an important paper whose author remains anonymous but criticizes the established Reagan administration policy. This paper was originally leaked to the *New York Times* in 1981. Other important documents include those prepared for the U.S. Congress generally and the U.S. House Committee on Intelligence specifically concerning El Salvador, the *Report of the President's National Bipartisan Commission on Central America*, prepared for the Reagan administration in the early 1980s, the report of the North American Congress on Latin America, an important U.S. State Department "white paper" from the very early weeks of the Reagan administration, documents of the U.S. Immigration and Naturalization Service concerning refugees from the Salvadoran war zone, and various publicly available reports on El Salvador in the 1980s from the U.S. State Department, U.S. Defense Department, and the United Nations.

Assorted humanitarian, relief, and "human rights" groups also compiled valuable documentation concerning the situation in El Salvador during the 1980s. Such sources include Amnesty International, Americas Watch, Human Rights Watch, the International Red Cross, the American Civil Liberties Union, and agencies sponsored by various religious denominations, including the Catholic Church, both in Latin America and in the United States, the National Council of Churches, and the U.S. Friends Committee. Detailed reports were made available by these organizations based on the first hand observations and experiences of relief workers operating within or close to the war zone and those dealing with refugees displaced by the war.

Additional primary sources include the personal memoirs and other writings of persons directly involved in the formulation of policy, both in the United States and in El Salvador. Among the more important of these are the works of former US Secretary of State Alexander Haig, former U.S. Secretary of State George Shultz, former President of El Salvador Jose Napolean Duarte, former US Ambassador to the United Nations Jeane Kirkpatrick and former U.S. Ambassador to El Salvador Robert White. A substantial amount of material is also available from journalists and others operating directly from El Salvador during the time of the war.

Given the controversial nature of the Reagan administration's Central America policy and the disastrous nature of the Salvadoran civil war, a voluminous amount of secondary sources are available pertaining to the topics.

El Salvador - A War by Proxy

Many academic and journalistic critiques of the policies and actions of the various parties to the war were produced during the 1980s and these writings predictably span the entire spectrum of scholarly as well as ideological and polemical outlooks. Likewise, these events were subject to widespread news coverage by the international press and much material is available from the archives of leading journalistic outlets.

1   *CIA World Fact Book*. Accessed March 22, 2008. Archived at https://www. cia.gov/library/publications/the-world-factbook/index.html

2   William Blum, *Killing Hope: U.S. Military and CIA Interventions Since World War II* (Monroe, Maine: Common Courage Press, 2004), pp. 357-358

3   Blum, pp. 356-357

4   Arthur Jones, "El Salvador Revisited: A Look at Declassified State Department Documents - Some of What U.S. Government Knew - and When It Knew It", *National Catholic Reporter*, September 23, 1994.

5   Marc Cooper and Gregory Goldin, "*Interview With Jose Napolean Duarte*", *Playboy*, Chicago, November, 1984, p. 73.

6   David Moreno, *U.S. Foreign Policy in Central America: The Endless Debate* (Miami: Florida University Press, 1990), pp. 82-88

7   Moreno, pp. 85-86.

8   Blum, p. 352.

9   Stephen Webre, *Jose Napolean Duarte and the Christian Democratic Party in Salvadoran Politics, 1960-1972* (Louisiana State University Press, Baton Rouge, La., 1979), p. 57.

10   John Lewis Gaddis, Strategies of Containment: *A Critical Appraisal of American National Security Policy During the Cold War*. Revised and Expanded Edition (Oxford and New York: Oxford University Press, 2005)

11   Gaddis Smith, *Morality, Reason and Power: American Diplomacy in the Carter Years,* (New York, Hill and Wang, 1986), pp. 241, 247.

12   William Blum, *Killing Hope: U.S. Military and CIA Interventions Since World War II* (Monroe, Maine: Common Courage Press, 2004); Noam Chomsky, *Deterring Democracy* (New York: Hill and Wang, 1992); Noam Chomsky, *Turning the Tide: U.S. Intervention in Central America and the Struggle for Peace* (Boston: South End Press, 1985); Alexander, Cockburn, *Corruptions of Empire: Life Studies and the Reagan Era* (Haymarket Press, 1988); Michael Parenti, *The Sword and the Dollar: Imperialism, Revolution and the Arms Race* (St. Martin's Press, 1988); Howard Zinn, *Declarations of Independence: Cross-Examining American Ideology* (Perennial Publishers,

Comments on Primary Sources

1991).

Scott, Peter Dale and Jonathan Marshall. *Cocaine Politics: Drugs, Armies and the CIA in Central America.* University of California Press, 1991; Zinn, Howard. *Declarations of Independence: Cross-Examining American Ideology.* Perennial Publishers, 1991.

13   Blum, p. 366.

Chapter 1

Expropriation, Hegemony and Repression

The Historic Roots of the Salvadoran Conflict

In 1931, El Salvador was described by the United States attaché for Central American military affairs, Major R. A. Harris, as "very much like France was before its revolution, Russia before its revolution and Mexico before its revolution." Harris predicted that a revolution would eventually come to El Salvador as well with the additional prescient comment that "when it comes it will be a bloody one." He observed that there was "practically no middle class" and "roughly ninety percent of the wealth of the country is held by about one half of one percent of the population. Thirty or forty families own nearly everything in the country. They live in almost regal splendor with many attendants, send their children to Europe or the United States to be educated, and spend money lavishly (on themselves). The rest of the population has practically nothing." [1]

This pattern of severe social and economic underdevelopment continued virtually unabated over the next half century until revolution and civil war finally erupted. By the end of the 1970s, El Salvador had achieved the most grossly disproportionate distribution of wealth and income of all Latin American nations, an impressive statistic indeed.

Nearly seventy percent of the Salvadoran people were peasants. In 1978, adult literacy rates were only sixty-three percent for the nation as a whole, thirty percent for rural people, and barely ten percent for the peasant population itself. Only eight percent of rural children had access to even primary-level education. At the beginning of the civil war, only one physician existed for every 3,592 persons, with two-thirds of these located in the capital city of San Salvador. The two provinces that became the center of revolutionary activities, Chalatenango and

Morazan, possessed only one physician per 90,000 people.[2] The *New York Times* reporter Raymond Bonner, who visited and wrote about El Salvador extensively during the time prior to the civil war and the early years of the war, described the extreme class polarization to be found in Salvadoran society:

> I would come to the posh residential districts. On one side of the street are the expensive, modern houses, with swimming pools and well-tended gardens. On the other side are the ravines...Into them are plunged shanties and shacks, where extended families share the dirt. From their porches or glassed-in dining rooms, the wealthy can gaze out across... the expanse, across the top of the ravines. The misery beneath them is not visible. The (capital city of San Salvador) is ringed by a belt of squalid, noisy, grimy neighborhoods... where merchants peddle their wares...and women spread fruits and vegetables on the ground in open-air markets.

> A paved road leading south from the capital is for the convenience of those who can afford to go to the Pacific coast beaches, where the wealthy have their second homes on cliffs with views that would be envied by Californians... but get off the paved roads...and you enter a semi feudal society. It's a time warp. It looks like Appalachia or the American West in the 1800s. Rural Salvadoran villages are built around a central square. The whitewashed Catholic Church dominates one side. The other three sides are continuous rows of dull brown mud walls, with veneers of thin plaster, divided into family quarters, a pharmacy, a general store, and the local Alcoholics Anonymous. Weeds grow out of the tiles over eaves that angle down over wooden walkways. Outside these villages are clusters of mud hovels, bisected by rutted dirt paths.

> Barefoot boys and men wearing chaps ride horses with bulky wood saddles. In the dry season, the dirt, ground to a fine dust, is suffocating.

During the rainy periods oozing mud makes each step an effort. Filthy naked children with painfully distended bellies, festering eyes, and open sores wander among grunting pigs, stinking garbage, scrawny dogs, and flies. Three out of four Salvadoran peasant children suffer from malnutrition. Their mothers and sisters trudge for an hour or more to the nearest source of water to haul it in gourd-shaped plastic containers balanced on their heads. Only one-fourth of the rural population has access to safe water, and a mere 17 percent has adequate means of waste disposal. Diarrhea, not cancer or heart disease, is the major cause of death.[3]

El Salvador's level of industrialization in the 1970s was rather minimal. The Salvadoran economy was still very much agrarian in nature. A handful of elite landowners controlled nearly eighty percent of the arable land. Wages for agricultural workers typically ranged between $1 and $3 per day. Most land cultivation was oriented towards the production of export crops while the peasants engaged in subsistence farming on small, hillside plots on the periphery of the great plantations. In 1977, the nutritional standards of the Salvadoran people were the second lowest in Latin America, barely above those of the Bolivians, not as high as those of the Haitians and way below those of the Cubans. Malnutrition was the cause of one half of all deaths of Salvadoran children ages five and under. Ten percent of all peasant children would die before the age of one year.

The extreme class divisions found in El Salvador in the 1970s had their roots in the nation's distant past. The indigenous people of El Salvador, known as the Pipil Indians, had been conquered nearly four hundred and fifty years earlier by the Spanish conquistadors. It was not until 1821 that El Salvador claimed its independence from Spain, initially petitioning for statehood status from the United States, and it is not fully known how this request was handled by the American government of the time. El Salvador became an independent nation in 1839. The system of land ownership in Salvadoran society was communal in nature as late as the end of the eighteenth century with ownership rights relegated to individual towns and Pipil villages. The primary agricultural products produced by the peasants were cattle, indigo, corn, beans and coffee. The Pipil were essentially practicing a type of community self-sufficiency.

As the international market for coffee expanded, some of the wealthier and more powerful merchants and landowners began pressuring the Salvadoran government to intervene into the economic structures of the nation in such a way as to make the accumulation of personal wealth more rapid through the establishment of larger, private plantations with a more greatly regimented labor force. Consequently, the government began to destroy the traditional system of property rights held by the towns and villages in order to establish individual plantations owned by those from the privileged classes who already possessed the means of acquiring credit. This change was implemented in several steps. In 1846, landowners with more than 5,000 coffee bushes were granted immunity from paying export duties for seven years and from paying taxes for a ten year period. Plantations owned by the Salvadoran government were also transferred to politically connected private individuals. In 1881, the communal land rights the Pipil had possessed for centuries were rescinded, making self-sufficiency for the Indians impossible. The government subsequently refused to grant even subsistence plots to the Pipil as the Salvadoran state was now fully under the control of the large plantation owners. This escalating economic repression was met with resistance and five separate peasant rebellions occurred during the late nineteenth century.[4]

The Salvadoran civil war of the 1980s had its roots in a failed uprising nearly fifty years earlier, a 1932 peasant rebellion that was thoroughly crushed. By this point, El Salvador's coffee plantations, called *fincas*, were producing ninety-five percent of the Country's export product and were controlled by a tiny oligarchy of landowning families.

Augustin Farabundo Marti emerged as the leader of a popular resistance movement. Himself a child of El Salvador's ruling class, Farabundo Marti had become a political radical during his time as a student at the university in San Salvador. His radical activities led to conflicts with the authorities and he subsequently journeyed to Guatemala and then the United States where he became involved with the Anti-Imperialist League, an organization of Americans, some of them rather prominent, who were opposed to interference in the internal politics of Latin America by the United States government.

Forced to flee the United States because his political activities were considered subversive by the American authorities, he subsequently became a guerrilla fighter in Nicaragua along with the famed Augusto Cesar Sandino and was a founder of El Salvador's *Socorro Rojo Internacional* ("Red Aid Society"). The Internacional moved towards an alliance with El Salvador's Communist Party. The Communists subsequently led a mass demonstration in the capital city of San Salvador on May Day of 1930. More than 80,000 workers, peasants and students participated and the purpose of the protest was to demand a minimum wage for workers on the agricultural plantations along with unemployment compensation. The government responded by prohibiting public protests, strikes by labor organizations, and the publication of subversive literature. Farabundo Marti and other protest leaders continued to try to organize opposition to the landowners and the government over the next twenty months until Marti was finally arrested on January 19, 1932. On January 22, a peasant uprising took place in Sonsonate Province, located in the Western region of El Salvador where the economic and political oppression of the agricultural workers was the most severe. Marti was executed by firing squad on February 1.[5]

An important scholarly work on the 1932 rebellion was produced in 1971 by an American historian, Thomas P. Anderson, author of the book *Matanza: El Salvador's Communist Revolt of 1932*. Anderson attempted to recreate the events of the rebellion based on the first person accounts of survivors. Anderson estimated that roughly one hundred persons, mostly soldiers, were killed by the rebels during the initial uprising. El Salvador's then-military dictator, General Maximiliano Hernandez Martinez, a strong believer in reincarnation, remarked, "It is a greater crime to kill an ant than a man, for when a man dies he becomes reincarnated, while an ant dies forever." He retaliated by slaughtering an estimated 30,000 peasants, mostly Pipil Indians.[6] The aftermath of the *matanza*, or "massacre", was described as follows:

> Roadways and drainage ditches were littered with bodies, gnawed at by buzzards and pigs. Hotels were raided; individuals with blond hair were dragged out and killed as suspected Russians. Men were tied thumb to thumb, then executed, tumbling into mass graves they had first been forced to dig. General Hernandez Martinez's name and methods have been venerated by (subsequent) military death squads operating in El Salvador...Subsequent military governments in El Salvador have deliberately tried to erase from the country's history the brutality of 1932. The National Library has been purged of all records, including newspapers, that covered the period of the revolt. Government files have been destroyed.[7]

In the half century that followed, a series of governments ruled El Salvador with an iron fist and were resolutely resistant to reform. A student rebellion in 1960 was likewise met with brutal repression, including the murder of a university librarian and the rape of several female students by the police, and the subsequent gunning down of student protestors. A group of reform-minded military officers initiated a coup in October of that year, but were overthrown after only three months with the counterrevolution being supported by the United States. Throughout the 1950s, 1960s and 1970s aid from the United States was used to build up the Salvadoran National Guard, police, and intelligence services, and it was from these forces that the leadership of the notorious "death squads" that massacred suspected opponents of the regime in the 1970s and early 1980s were drawn.[8]

In the latter part of the twentieth century, the economic situation of El Salvador's poorest citizens was arguably the most desperate in all of Latin America. Though token opposition was allowed throughout the 1960s and 1970s, genuine opposition parties, such as those calling for agrarian or banking reform, were banned and in 1972, when a center-left coalition led by Jose Napolean Duarte achieved electoral victory, the election results were nullified by the Central Electoral Board in a questionable ruling. Subsequent elections in the 1970s were accompanied by intimidation of voters and opposition candidates by the military and the police and, elections aside, the real power in the country remained in the hands of the so-called "Fourteen Families," the oligarchs who dominated Salvadoran agriculture, industry and finance and kept the country in a semi-feudal state.[9] Hundreds of protesters were massacred by the security forces during a demonstration against electoral fraud in 1977. This kind of repression began to escalate in the late 1970s and the opposition likewise resorted to more militant tactics, viewing electoral efforts as futile and turning increasingly towards strikes, occupations, even more militant demonstrations, bombings, kidnappings and assassinations. The government and the Salvadoran oligarchy in return unleashed "death squads" (right-wing paramilitary groups) against the opposition including political parties, labor unions, peasant organizations, and officials, clerics and lay workers of the Catholic Church. The American CIA assisted in gathering intelligence on opponents of the regime who were sometimes subsequently murdered by the death squads.[10]

In 1979, yet another group of reformist military officers staged a coup, but were quickly overwhelmed by the wider military establishment, pressure from the United States, and their own inexperience. [11] Meanwhile, the civilian officials within the regime were unable to exercise any kind of effective authority over the military itself. All of the civilian members of the government had resigned by January 1980 and casualties continued to increase in clashes between the security forces and anti-government protesters. The Minister of Education announced his resignation on television and proclaimed his allegiance to the emerging guerrilla insurgency. On January 22, 1980, 21 protesters were killed by the security forces and 120 were wounded. On March 17, 54 people were killed during a general strike. Oscar Romero, the Archbishop of El Salvador gave his last sermon that month, begging US President Jimmy Carter, and appealing in the context of "Christian to Christian," to end to all aid to the Salvadoran regime. He was assassinated the next day. The security forces attacked the Archbishop's funeral with a bomb and rifle fire, killing 40 people.[12] Years later, President Jose Napoleon Duarte would reveal that the murder of Archbishop Romero had been orchestrated by a Salvadoran army officer by the name of Roberto D'Aubuisson, the known leader of the right-wing paramilitary "death squads." At one point, D'Aubussion said to a group of German journalists, "You Germans were very intelligent. You realized that the Jews were responsible for the spread of communism, and you began to kill them."[13] It was known to the American CIA that D'Aubuisson was behind Romero's assassination "no later than one year" after the murder transpired.[14]

The Carter administration pushed for land reform in El Salvador during the early months of 1980. Similar efforts had been advocated by the U.S. elsewhere in Latin America, primarily as a means of defusing radical insurgencies by at least partially addressing the social and economic problems that gave rise to them. Critics typically dismissed these as a cosmetic, face-saving tactic whose purpose was to make U.S. client states appear to be more benevolent and open to reform than they actually were.[15] Even the feeble attempts at land reform enacted by the Salvadoran regime under U.S. pressure failed. El Salvador's landed oligarchy would simply expel peasant farmers altogether rather than comply with land reform measures. Pretended reforms were sometimes used as a means of identifying influential community leaders who would then be marked for death.[16] Within a few days after the attempted land reform began, seven leaders of peasant organizations were assassinated.[17]

Historic Relations Between the United States and El Salvador

The deplorable political and economic conditions of El Salvador in the late 1970s had their roots not only in the nation's history as a Spanish colony and subsequent internal politics following the achievement of independence in the early nineteenth century, but also in El Salvador's post-independence status as a client state of the United States. After independence, El Salvador was initially part of the five-nation Central American Federation, along with Nicaragua, Guatemala, Honduras and Costa Rica, a political body that lasted until 1838, when each of the five members of the federation became an independent nation-state. Panama became a sixth independent Central American nation in 1906 and Belize followed in 1981 after being granted independence from Great Britain. The United States displayed an interest in the Central American nations as far back as the period immediately following independence. The establishment of trade relations through the mutual reduction of tariffs, import duties and other trade barriers was an early American objective that, while innocuous enough on its face, had the effect of throwing the weight of American diplomacy behind rival factions within the Central American nations and aggravating conflict within the domestic politics of those nations.[18]

The United States also sought to prevent the expansion of influence in Central America by the major European powers of the era, particularly Great Britain, while expanding American influence. It was, after all, the era of the famed "Monroe Doctrine" and "Manifest Destiny". America's efforts to curtail the British presence in the region enjoyed infrequent success, and the British Empire continued to exercise a great deal of political, economic and military power in Central America. Above all, the United States desired the construction of a canal through Central America for the sake of establishing a trade route connecting the Atlantic and Pacific Oceans, an ambition that was eventually achieved some decades later with the construction of the Panama Canal.

An important figure in the history of relations between the United States and the Central American nations was William Walker, a native of San Francisco, who organized a private army of mercenaries, gold prospectors and other adventurers and ne'er-do-wells in 1849 and subsequently invaded El Salvador's nearby neighboring state of Nicaragua.

A Nicaraguan political figure, General Francisco Castellon, had made an arrangement with a San Francisco businessman, Byron Cole, for the recruitment of a private mercenary army in exchange for land grants. Cole then turned to Walker to carry out the task of the invasion and Walker eventually landed in Nicaragua with an army of 2,500 fighters carried on ships owned by the famed American financier Cornelius Vanderbilt. Walker's force went on to conquer Nicaragua with Walker eventually installing himself as president through a fraudulent election. Among Walker's acts as "president" were to legalize slavery and dispossess native Nicaraguans of their land rights. Vanderbilt then lobbied the United States Senate for a federal contract to build a canal in Nicaragua. The scheme eventually failed when Walker turned on Vanderbilt in favor of some of his rivals and former associates, and when the other Central American nations declared war on the Walker government. Incensed by Walker's treachery, Vanderbilt used his political influence to prevent American troops from coming to Walker's aid. Walker fled to the United States, and then organized yet another expedition to Central America, this time to Honduras. He was eventually captured by a British naval ship. The British turned Walker over to the Honduran authorities, who then executed him in 1860. The

Walker episode served to create a substantial level of distrust of the United States by the Central American nations.[19]

In the late nineteenth century, the United States began to gradually abandon its traditional foreign policy isolationism and started to build an empire of its own. As American economic power grew, so did the desire of American elites to exercise greater influence on an international level. Under the leadership of President William McKinley, the United States acquired numerous island territories in the Pacific and in the Caribbean. These included Puerto Rico, Cuba, the Philippine Islands, Hawaii, Samoa, and others. It was during this period that the United States began developing its client-state system in Central America.

Traditional United States Foreign Policy in Latin America

The principal motivations behind the construction of U.S. foreign policy towards Central America during this early period of the client-state system were the continued interest in the building of a canal joining the Pacific and Atlantic Oceans, the desire for foreign export markets (motivated in part by the economic depression of the 1890s), the increased ability of the United States to eclipse the influence of Spain, England and other European powers in the Western Hemisphere due in part to increased economic and military capabilities, and the belief that U.S. geopolitical and military security was greatly enhanced through the American domination of the region. In the years immediately preceding the beginning of the First World War, the U.S. engaged in the direct military occupation of Nicaragua, Haiti, and the Dominican Republic.[20]

At the time the United States was developing its client-state system in Central America, the region was experiencing substantial economic growth, largely to due the success of these nations at producing coffee and bananas as export crops. It was the elite sectors of Central American societies, particularly landowners, politicians, and merchants, who most heavily profited from the growing subordination of the nations of Central America to the interests of the United States. The United States intervened militarily in Central America more than twenty times between 1901 and 1933 for the sake of maintaining or installing regimes in the region that were favorable to American economic or geopolitical objectives. The outbreak of the First World War cemented American dominance of Central America as all of the European rivals to the United States necessarily focused their attention and resources on the prosecution of their respective war efforts. Resistance to American domination of Central America began to grow during the period prior to World War Two, both within the domestic United States and in Central America itself. What came to be known as America's policy of "dollar diplomacy" was sharply criticized by U.S. labor radicals, trade union activists, Socialist leaders, Democratic Party politicians, and right-wing Republican isolationists. Mexico underwent a revolution in 1917 and rebellion broke out in Nicaragua in the early 1930s under the leadership of Augusto Cesar Sandino. Other Latin American countries, notably Argentina, pushed for the creation of a Pan-American Union whose purpose would be the assertion of Latin American interests against U.S. imperialism and a majority of the nations of Latin America joined the Union. Domestic unrest also began to develop in some Central American nations with new labor unions and political parties representing the working classes and urban middle classes being formed.[21]

The Great Depression brought with it President Franklin D. Roosevelt's Good Neighbor Policy with regards to Central America. The export-model economies of these nations and the domination of the plantation oligarchies were challenged by the international depression. As a consequence, in both El Salvador and Guatemala, the military become increasingly powerful in its own right as the traditional oligarchies became more dependent on the military for the repression of internal dissent. American military concerns about the possibility of the establishment of

Axis bases in Latin America during World War Two brought the relationship between the United States and the military establishments of Central America closer together. Though the Good Neighbor Policy ostensibly favored greater autonomy for Central American countries, the pressures of the war actually brought about an increased American presence as "U.S. diplomats, military officials, FBI agents, technical advisers, and private businesspeople swarmed through the region in unprecedented numbers." [22] The U.S. organized a coup against the uncooperative government of Panama in 1941.

The end of World War Two left the United States as the world's premiere power, both in the military and economic realms. Efforts by the United States to incorporate the Latin American nations into a wider alliance brought U.S. interests into conflict with local and regional efforts at political and economic reform. U.S. policy makers were particularly concerned about the participation of Communists in such reform efforts, though actual Communists were usually only peripheral players within wider reform movements. A particularly significant incident during the early Cold War period was the role of the United States in undermining the populist-nationalist, democratic-reformist regime of Guatemala's Jacobo Arbenz in 1954. The official U.S position was that the Arbenz government had fallen under the control of Communism and had been overthrown in a popular revolution. The reality was that the Arbenz regime was more moderate and less left-wing than certain other pro-American governments in Latin America and had been brought down by a military coup in which American agents had played a major role. The most plausible motive for the overturning of the Arbenz government by the Americans is the threat to certain domestic American business interests, particularly those of the United Fruit Company, a company with substantial representation in the uppermost levels of the Truman and Eisenhower administrations, posed by the efforts at agricultural reform instituted by Arbenz and the willingness of his regime to act independently of Washington, which had the effect of undermining the client-state system. [23]

The Kennedy Administration's Alliance for Progress ostensibly sought to enhance stability in Latin America through the promotion of political and economic reform. However, actual attempts at such reform were relatively feeble given both the opposition of the Latin American ruling classes, vested interests within the United States exercising influence over U.S. policy in the region and fears about undermining security on the part of American foreign policy officials. The reformist aspects of the Alliance for Progress were never pursued consistently. Instead, the principal focus was on the prevention of the creation of new Soviet allies of the Cuban variety in Latin America and on protecting U.S. business interests. Consequently, the strength of the local oligarchies and the military establishments within the Central American nations actually increased under the Alliance. This in turn led to an increase in domestic repression in those countries.[24]

By the 1970s, U.S. influence had declined somewhat in Latin America, partially due to the attention given by U.S. administrations to foreign policy considerations elsewhere, such as Asia or the Middle East. At this point, authoritarian military regimes were the norm in Latin America and social and economic conditions were deteriorating considerably. The U.S. ignored Latin America throughout most of the decade prior to the onset of the Salvadoran civil war. The notable exception to this trend was the role of the Nixon government in overturning the left-wing democratic socialist regime of Chile's Salvador Allende and the subsequent installation of the military government of General Augusto Pinochet.[25] However, the American-organized coup against President Allende foreshadowed what was to come in the years ahead as Latin America, particularly the Central American nations, became increasingly important to U.S. policy makers by the end of the 1970s.

El Salvador - A War by Proxy

1   Raymond Bonner, *Weakness and Deceit: U.S. Policy and El Salvador* (New York: Times Books, 1984), p. 16

2   Bonner, p.17

3   Bonner, p.19

4   Bonner, pp.19-22

5   Bonner, pp.22-23

6   Thomas P. Anderson, *Matanza: El Salvador's Communist Revolt of 1932* (Lincoln: University of Nebraska Press, 1971), p. 134.

7   Bonner, p.23

8   New York Times, October 22, 1987, p. 11; American Civil Liberties Union and Americas Watch Committee, *Report on Human Rights in El Salvador* (New York: Vintage Books, 1982), p. 179-180, 189-197; James Dunkerley, *The Long War: Dictatorship and Revolution in El Salvador* (London: Junction Books, 1982), pp. 74-75; Michael McClintock, *The American Connection: State Terror and Popular Resistance in El Salvador* (London: Zed Books, 1985), pp. 135-137, 149; Jenny Pearce, Under the Eagle (London, 1982), pp. 214-216.

9   Robert Armstrong and Janet Shenk, *El Salvador: The Face of Revolution,* (London, 1982), pp. 50-87.

10   Allan Nairn, "Behind the Death Squads", *The Progressive* (Madison, Wisconsin), May 1984, pp. 1, 20-29.

11   Carolyn Forche, "The Road to Reaction in El Salvador", *The Nation* (New York), June 14, 1980, p. 712.

12   Blum, p. 355.

13   Blum, p. 356.

14   Ibid.

15   Michael McClintock, *The American Connection: State Terror and Popular Resistance in El Salvador* (London: Zed Books, 1985), pp. 266-271.

16   NACLA Report on the Americas, "*El Salvador: A Revolution Brews*" (North American Conference on Latin America, New York, July-August 1980), p. 17.

17   Philip Wheaton, *Agrarian Reform in El Salvador* (Ecumenical Program for Interamerican Communication and Action, Washington, D.C., 1980), p. 13.

18   John H. Coatsworth, *Central America and the United States: The Clients and the Colussus* (New York: Twayne Publishers, 1994), pp. 1, 24-25.

19   Karl Bermann, *Under the Big Stick: Nicaragua and the United States Since 1948* (Boston: South End Press, 1989), p. 73; William Walker, The War in Nicaragua (Mobile, Alabama: S. H. Goetzel, 1860).

20   Walter Lafeber, *The New Empire: A Interpretation of American Expansion,*

Expropriation, Hegemony and Repression

1860-1898 (Ithaca, New York: Cornell University Press, 1963); Thomas M. Leonard, *Central America and the United States: The Search for Stability* (Athens: University of Georgia Press, 1991); Alfred Thayer Mahan, *The Interest of America in Sea Power* (Boston: Little and Brown, 1897); Ernest R. May, *Imperial Democracy: The Emergence of America as a Great Power* (New York: Harcourt, Brace & World, 1961); William Appleman Williams, *The Roots of the Modern American Empire* (New York: Random House, 1969).

21   Coatsworth, pp. 39-41.

22   Coatsworth, pp. 48.

23   Coatsworth, pp. 67-74.

24   Coatsworth, pp. 117-120.

25   Coatsworth, p. 160.

Chapter 2

The Retreat Into Barbarism

The Carter Administration, Foreign Policy and Latin America

When the administration of Jimmy Carter assumed power in 1977, a substantially greater interest was placed on Latin America than had been the case with the past few administrations. Carter's policies had four primary components. The first three of these were the negotiation of a new Panama Canal Treaty, a greater emphasis on "human rights" and efforts to distance the United States from Latin American governments with atrocious human rights records, and increased aid to impoverished Latin American countries, particularly those of the Central American region. Lastly, the Carter administration wished to normalize relations with Cuba. All of these policies were part of a broader plan by the administration to restore American dominance in Latin America. [1]

Carter's greater interest in Latin American affairs than his predecessors was personal as well as political. As a southern planter by profession, he was experienced in business dealings in Latin America, spoke Spanish fluently, and had previously visited Mexico, Brazil, Colombia, Costa Rica and Argentina. He was also personally concerned about the horrendous human rights situations in many Latin American countries. Carter's efforts in this area initially brought about limited successes. The Carter government initially pushed for some modest reforms in Latin American countries and succeeded in obtaining a reduction in the use of torture by some of these regimes along with the release of some political prisoners. Carter's administration also pushed the government of Honduras to hold elections and allow civilian participation in politics. The number of signatory nations to the American Convention on Human

Rights increased from two in 1977 to fourteen in 1980. Cuba released 3,900 political prisoners and all of Paraguay's political prisoners were freed. Confirmed disappearances of political dissidents were reduced to zero in 1978 in both Chile and Uruguay. Disappearances of this kind were reduced by ninety percent in Argentina. The Carter administration's emphasis on democratization also helped to reduce electoral corruption in Peru and Ecuador. Carter's initial success won him much praise, including expressions of sympathy from political opponents. For example, the conservative journalist William F. Buckley, Jr. initially attacked Carter's pro-human rights policies as naïve and ineffective, but subsequently reversed his position, observing that "the advertisement by American agencies official and non-official, of the plight of missing persons as often as not had concrete results. Pressure was felt by the criminal abductors. The man scheduled for execution was, often, merely kept in jail." [2]

The combined effects of economic decline and increased repression in some countries despite improvements in others created political chaos in Central America on a level that the Carter administration had not expected and was not prepared for. Popular discontent in the region was at an all-time high. In 1977, the Carter administration temporarily shut off military aid to Guatemala and El Salvador. However, this policy became self-defeating as economic aid to these countries continued with the aid funds simply being shifted to military purposes. Overall U.S. aid to the Central American countries increased by 9.2 percent during the Carter administration over what it had been during the administrations of Richard Nixon and Gerald Ford. [3]

The administration's ambitions were similar to the stated aims of the Alliance for Progress in that they sought to reduce the potential for radical upheaval and to curb anti-American sentiment by pushing for modest social, economic and political reforms. The success of this light-handed approach varied from nation to nation, but its failure was most evident in Nicaragua, where the United States was heavily identified with the hated Somoza regime, and in El Salvador, because it was essentially abandoned after the fall of Somoza at the hands of the Sandinista revolution in Nicaragua due to fears of a similar revolution in El Salvador.

Any effort to dissect American foreign policy towards El Salvador during the course of the civil war must take into account the effect of the Sandinista revolution in Nicaragua on the mindset of American policy makers. The extremely corrupt and incompetent regime of Anastasio Somoza Debayle was overthrown by the Sandinista National Liberation Front on July 19, 1979. The Somoza government had so alienated Nicaraguans from virtually all political or class backgrounds that its demise became inevitable. The Carter administration was surprised by the rapid downfall of Somoza and pressured him to initiate reforms for the purpose of preventing a Sandinista seizure of power. In 1978, Somoza announced that he would step down as President in 1981 but his opponents saw this as a ruse and a delaying tactic employed for the purpose of pacifying the opposition and strengthening Somoza's own power base. The Carter administration then sought to replace Somoza with a new set of leaders who would be "moderate" and "pro-American" in their rhetoric and policies. Somoza responded by announcing a set of very modest reforms, which earned him a letter of commendation from Carter, an act that outraged Nicaraguans, who believed Carter was simply playing along with Somoza's stalling efforts. Somoza attempted to trap the Carter administration into a situation where there was no alternative between his regime and the FSLN. The Carter administration then formally suspended military assistance to Somoza (a dubious act as armaments already on order were delivered anyway) and pressured Latin American countries to end aid to the Sandinistas. When it finally became apparent that Somoza was immune to pressures to implement reforms capable of defusing the situation, the United States eventually ended all aid to Nicaragua and recalled its ambassador, focusing instead on pushing other nations to end support to the Sandinistas so as to prevent their eventual taking of power. [4]

Once Somoza had been overthrown, the Carter administration adopted a policy meant to prevent a repeat of the events of the Cuban revolution twenty years earlier, where U.S. heavy handedness had pushed the revolutionaries into an alliance with the Soviet Union. Consequently, Nicaragua was offered "cordial" relations with the United States, economic aid, and the encouragement of assistance from private investors, American allies, and transnational agencies such as the International Monetary Fund. Meanwhile, the Sandinista revolutionaries sought to strengthen their own position by using their popularity to mobilize Nicaraguan public support for their government, develop functional and efficient military and police forces, and develop relationships with other Latin American countries and with nations outside the Western hemisphere. The United States offered to provide military training to the Nicaraguan forces, but this offer was ignored, as Nicaraguan leaders were fearful of a repeat of past U.S. efforts to subvert reformist or revolutionary governments in Latin America by means of a military coup. Instead, the Sandinistas sought to create safety for themselves by purging the pro-U.S. elements from the new government, and by developing ties to nations hostile to the United States, particularly Cuba, as well as U.S. allies such as France. [5]

The Carter Administration and the Beginning of the Salvadoran Civil War

A somewhat neglected aspect of U.S. foreign policy towards El Salvador concerns the role of the Carter administration and its support for the Salvadoran regime in the late 1970s and in the early months of the civil war in 1980 and 1981. To some degree this is understandable as most of the war period occurred during the same time as the Reagan and Bush administrations and these administrations were certainly more strident and bellicose in both their rhetoric and in their policies towards El Salvador, and towards the nations of Central America more generally. Yet much of the Carter administration's record on the question of El Salvador tarnishes Carter's reputation as a proponent and upholder of "human rights" considerably.

Early on, the Carter administration had criticized the lack of regard of the Salvadoran regime for human rights and hoped for a transition to a more democratic, civilian form of government. In Nicaragua, the business class had opposed Somoza's archaic feudal order, and had played a role in ousting his government. While the more pro-U.S. representatives of the business sector had been purged from the revolutionary government by the staunchly nationalistic Sandinistas, the FSLN regime retained a market-oriented economy (with the exception of quasi-feudal plantations that had been nationalized and converted into agricultural cooperatives) as opposed to a traditional Marxist, state-directed economy. However, in El Salvador the business class was divided, with the landowners and coffee exporters pitted against industrialists, manufacturers and other commercial interests of the kind associated with more modern "capitalist" economies. U.S. intelligence sources claimed that the emerging guerilla forces in El Salvador posed no significant threat to the regime. A similar claim was initially made concerning the Sandinista rebel forces in Nicaragua. After the Nicaraguan revolution in 1979, U.S. policy towards El Salvador began to reflect a harder line taken by the Carter administration. Crucially, decision-making authority concerning Central America passed from the State Department to the National Security Council and the Pentagon. The new policy had as its focus the prevention of the fall of another U.S. client state to revolutionary forces. This policy change was never publicly acknowledged as such acknowledgement might have alienated both Congress and the U.S. public, encouraged increased repression by the Salvadoran government, and driven the Salvadoran public towards greater support for the rebel forces. The U.S. foreign policy historian John H. Coatsworth provides an apt description of this shift in U.S. policy focus during this time:

> U.S. policy makers and diplomats continued to emphasize the need for an end to human rights abuses by the Salvadoran military and supported the creation of a civilian-led

government. Policy makers also continued to believe that the long-term stability depended on such changes. Whenever improving human rights or enhancing the power of civilian authorities threatened to destabilize the military, however, the United States backed off. Policy makers and diplomats denounced human rights abuses consistently over the four years of the Carter administration, but after mid-1979, as U.S. influence on the day-to-day activities of the Salvadoran regime reached a maximum, the United States began to appear not merely powerless to stop these abuses but complicit in their commission. [6]

Carlos Humberto Romero had been president of El Salvador during the early years of the Carter administration, having come to power in 1977 in an election tainted with electoral fraud. Though determined to crush any opposition to the regime, the Romero government temporarily drew back from its repressive efforts and put on a cosmetic image of reformism in order to secure U.S. loans that were being held back in part because of Carter's objections to his regime's disrespect for human rights. However, once the relaxing of repression produced an upswing of protest activity, Romero quickly clamped down, and even the smallest expressions of opposition to the state were met with violence. Romero attempted another relaxation of repression after the Sandinista revolution in Nicaragua as he became fearful that just as repression in that country had failed to prevent a revolution, so might El Salvador undergo a similar revolution. However, Romero's token efforts at reform proved useless and he was deposed in a coup in October of 1979. The coup was led in part by younger officers seeking at least some level of genuine reform, as well as more conservative officers who feared the incompetence of Romero had placed continued U.S. support at risk. While the United States welcomed the coup, very little support was given to the civilian members of the new government, nor was there any aid provided for any of its proposed reforms. Instead, the bulk of U.S. support was given to those members of the new regime whose first priority was the eradication of the rebel forces and the left-wing popular organizations with whom they were intertwined.[7]

All of the civilian members of the government installed in the October coup had resigned by January of 1980. In their place, the Christian Democratic Party was installed by the military as the civilian face of the regime due to U.S. insistence. The military fired upon a mass demonstration of 200,000 protestors on January 22, 1980. Between January of 1980 and January of 1981, the last year of Carter's term, more than 9,000 people were killed in acts of repression in El Salvador by the right-wing "death squads," including members of the supposedly ruling Christian Democratic Party. All but the most conservative members of the PDC either resigned or were expelled from the government. The army began forcing peasants suspected of offering support to the rebels into Vietnam-style "strategic hamlets."

Robert E. White was appointed as Carter's ambassador to El Salvador in March of 1980. He became an outspoken critic of the Salvadoran regime and ruling class and assumed considerable personal risks in doing so. Ambassador White later became an outspoken critic of Reagan administration policies in El Salvador as well, but what about the Carter administration? In an April 17, 2008 speech at a conference sponsored by the University of Texas, White discussed the role of the Catholic Church in pushing for political and economic reform in El Salvador. The leading figure in this effort was Archbishop Oscar Romero. White described his relationship with Romero during his time in El Salvador:

> I arrived on the scene as ambassador and quickly grasped that if U.S. policy to avoid a violent takeover by the left is to have any chance of working, that Romero was the key figure. If the United States could help the Salvadoran parties work out a peaceful agreement, only Monsignor Romero had the power to guarantee that agreement, because he was the only one trusted by the workers and campesinos.

I met almost immediately with Monsignor Romero, convinced him I understood the need for rapid change and that I would do everything I could to support him. I appointed an embassy officer to be in daily communication with the archbishop's office.[8]

White goes on to describe the reaction of the Carter administration to the aftermath of Romero's subsequent assassination:

Violence escalated, but the Carter administration still backed change. There was now a mixed civilian-military junta headed by Napoleon Duarte. With our support, land reform, nationalization of banks and other groundbreaking measures went forward. There was even some reduction in officially sponsored violence.

When Jimmy Carter lost the election to Ronald Reagan, there were wild celebrations in the rich barrios of Escalon and San Benito.

The Reagan transition team sent signals to the Salvadoran military that human rights were off the table and that any real dirty work the military had to do should be done while Carter was still in office.

In late November 1980, the military kidnapped and killed six political leaders of the non-violent FDR. In early January 1981, the military killed two American labor advisors and the Salvadoran chief of land reform.

On December 2, 1980, a detachment of soldiers from the Salvadoran National Guard kidnapped, raped and murdered four American citizens, three missionary nuns and a lay worker. For the next two weeks, El Salvador became the focus of worldwide attention. The murders of these four churchwomen had shocked and outraged the world. As soon as the administration of President Reagan took office, I received a phone call from the acting assistant secretary informing me that Secretary of State Alexander Haig requested I send him a telegram reporting that the Salvadoran military had initiated a serious investigation into the murders of the American churchwomen and that the investigation was making progress.

Why was Secretary of State Haig demanding such a telegram? Because when President Jimmy Carter learned of the murders, he reacted strongly, cutting off military and economic aid until the Salvadoran government demonstrated a good faith commitment to bring the murderers to justice.[9]

Is it really true that President Carter suspended assistance to the Salvadoran regime "until the Salvadoran government demonstrated a good faith commitment to bring the murderers to justice" or did the Carter administration continue to assist the regime in spite of its actions? White's own words betray this claim:

Let us stop for a moment and consider what was at stake. Once Secretary Haig received the kind of telegram he requested, he would use it to overcome congressional skeptics and massive military aid would begin to flow.

All I had to do was send in a telegram stating that the Salvadoran military high command had publicly denounced this senseless crime, that they had established a special high level commission to investigate the crime and that the president of the new commission had said he could promise a quick and satisfactory outcome.

Such a telegram would have been superficially accurate. It would have helped the Reagan administration to advance its new policy and it would have insured my promotion to positions of increasing responsibility.

Now, I am not one who sees every decision as a moral or ethical challenge. Over twenty five years I had developed the necessary elasticity of conscience to function effectively as a diplomat. I had, on more than one occasion, shaded the truth in order to give a policy time to work or had been somewhat less than candid in order to protect secrets.

In this case, however, Secretary Haig was asking me to affirm what I knew to be false, to use official channels to lie to my own government.

Within the hour, I had sent in a telegram stating that my embassy's reporting over the past six weeks had provided ample proof that the Salvadoran military had killed the four women, that once the bodies had been discovered, the Salvadoran high command had begun a massive cover-up designed to protect the guilty, that there was no investigation under way and that we could expect nothing from the Salvadoran military high command except a continuing cover-up.

Throughout history, diplomats have faced the problem of policy makers who would prefer not to know inconvenient facts that might undercut established policy. All classic texts on diplomacy warn the professional foreign service officer against telling the government what it "would like to hear, rather than what they ought to know." To fall into the practice of withholding information or distorting reports, says one commentator, "is to commit a disloyal act against one's own government."

As an example to others, I was immediately fired as ambassador to El Salvador and, soon after that, forced from the Foreign Service. Three other career diplomats serving in Central America refused to compromise their principles and also lost their careers. [10]

Ambassador White's ability to focus on considerations beyond his immediate professional self-interest may command respect, yet by his own admission the Salvadoran government was not only failing to make satisfactory progress concerning the human rights issues raised by the Carter administration, but was in fact working to undermine any effective efforts at addressing those concerns. Further, the Salvadoran regime's obscurantism on these matters was still evident at the time of the Reagan administration's coming to power. If indeed, as White has stated, the policy of the Carter administration had been one of "cutting off military and economic aid until the Salvadoran government demonstrated a good faith commitment to bring the murderers to justice," why did President Carter order that "$10 million dollars in military aid along with additional American advisers" be given to the Salvadoran regime during the final days of Carter's presidential term in January 1981? [11]

The Salvadoran civil war is associated with the Reagan administration, but it was well underway during the final period of the Carter administration. The Carter administration had a public image of commitment to peace and "human rights" and Carter has maintained this image for himself in the decades since his leaving office. Foreign policy decisions made by Carter and officials of his administration during 1980 were crucial to the future course of the Salvadoran war. Were it not for these decisions, the war might not have escalated to the level of intensity that it eventually did. It is also quite likely that the level of internal repression in El Salvador would not have reached the level observed in that country during the early 1980s. The Carter administration had full knowledge of the kinds of repression pursued by the Salvadoran government, having been repeatedly warned of such by the United States Ambassador to El Salvador Robert White, by pleas from Archbishop Oscar Romero to end American aid to El Salvador's regime, and by the protests of members of various American religious communities involved in relief efforts in El Salvador. Conventional intelligence and diplomatic sources also issued such warnings. The primary motivation of the Carter administration appears to have been fear of the loss of another U.S. client state in Central America similar to the prior loss of Nicaragua to the Sandinista revolution in 1979, which the Carter administration had initially tried to gain control of and then backed away from when it became clear Washington was not going to be able to direct the course of the revolution.

The true nature of the Carter administration's policy concerning El Salvador is of immense importance given Carter's reputation, both during his term as President and in subsequent decades, as a champion of "human rights". The journalists Jeff Cohen and Norman Solomon observed that "during his presidency, Carter proclaimed human rights to be 'the soul of our foreign policy.' Although many journalists promoted that image, the reality was quite different." [12]

Indeed, Carter's El Salvador policy was not an aberration or deviation from his administration's ostensible commitment to human rights as a cornerstone of foreign policy but was in fact a reflection of the Carter administration's normal habit of disregarding human rights considerations when such concerns came into conflict with the wider (and rather broadly defined) geopolitical objectives of United States foreign policy. Cohen and Solomon point out that upon assuming office in 1977, Carter increased military aid to the Indonesian regime that was at the time pursuing a campaign of near genocide against the Timorese.[13] Carter also continued to support the Iranian regime of Shah Mohammed Reza Pahlavi even to the point of toasting the Shah during his visit to the White House. [14] In Central America, the Carter administration supported not only the Salvadoran regime but also supported the regime of Nicaraguan dictator Anastasio Somoza until it became clear the end of his reign was inevitable. In Guatemala — again contrary to enduring myth — major U.S. military shipments to bloody tyrants never ended." [15] Perhaps most astonishingly of all, the Carter administration provided covert assistance to the Khmer Rouge regime of Cambodia's Pol Pot. The British journalist John Pilger observed:

Although the Khmer Rouge government ("Democratic Kampuchea") had ceased to exist in January 1979, its representatives were allowed to continue occupying Cambodia's seat at the UN; indeed, the US, China and Britain insisted on it. Meanwhile, a Security Council embargo on Cambodia compounded the suffering of a traumatised nation, while the Khmer Rouge in exile got almost everything it wanted. In 1981, President Jimmy Carter's national security adviser, Zbigniew Brzezinski, said: "I encouraged the Chinese to support Pol Pot." The US, he added, "winked publicly" as China sent arms to the Khmer Rouge. In fact, the US had been secretly funding Pol Pot in exile since January 1980. [16]

It was a rather interesting performance for an administration proclaiming its commitment to "human rights". A recent work by Itai Nartzizenfield Sneh examining the Carter administration's human rights policies offers this assessment:

In offering responses to human rights abuses, the (Carter administration) did not challenge incumbents, or distinguish between dictatorships and democracies, opting for stability over change. It could have supported alternative power bases such as opposition parties, grassroots organizations, and activists forced into exile. Instead, it exempted from human rights scrutiny most programs of military aid and food supplies to friendly regimes. The (Carter administration) could have suggested withholding aid to offending, friendly states by concentrating on long-term reforms. Instead, (administration human rights policy) asserted that objectives cannot be pursued simultaneously and evenly, preferring a case-by-case approach. The (Carter administration) did not propose mechanisms to judge performance of foreigners. By default, a preference for traditional U.S. interests prevailed...Without powerful procedures to reward good practices and penalize abusive countries, this policy was incomplete and ineffective. Ultimately, the United States abstained or voted against loan proposals to seventeen countries in multilateral organizations such as the International Monetary Fund, and the suspension of direct aid to Argentina, Bolivia, El Salvador, Guatemala, Haiti, Nicaragua, Paraguay, and Uruguay, which amounted to a limited censure given the scope of human rights abuses in Latin America.[17]

Another contemporary work by Kathryn Sikkink offers this evaluaton:

In the case of the Southern Cone, U.S. policy worked through both bilateral and multilateral channels; actions from regional and international organizations reinforced bilateral pressures. Moreover, factions within the Argentine and Uruguayan military governments, the so-called soft liners, decided to use U.S. and international pressures to pursue their own internal liberalization policy. Finally, U.S. human rights policy toward the Southern Cone countries was supported by the work of strong domestic human rights organizations and political parties with commitments to democracy and human rights.

In Central America, many of these conditions were missing. The active phase of Carter's human rights policies coincided with lower levels of human rights violations in Guatemala and in El Salvador. The escalating violations in 1979 and 1980 occurred during an upsurge in the numbers and the success of armed insurgent movements and coincided with the disenchantment phase of human rights policy. The beginnings of a full-fledged civil war in El Salvador and a major rural insurgency in Guatemala meant that U.S. human rights policy toward Guatemala and El Salvador was much less coherent and forceful. The priority of counterinsurgency goals led to the de-emphasis of human rights issues. No powerful groups existing within the Guatemalan military that could perceive a tactical advantage in responding to U.S. human rights pressures. In El Salvador, with the failure of the reformist military government of 1979, there was no soft-liner with the regime that could use U.S. pressure to bolster their own liberalization goals.[18]

El Salvador served as a crucible for the Carter administration's human rights policies and rhetoric. How strong was the administration's commitment to those policies? While not entirely ignoring such matters, the administration proved itself to be impotent when the question of human rights came up against other powerful interests and concerns, often virtually any other concern. Consequently, the tone was set for the discarding of human rights considerations altogether by the subsequent Reagan administration.

1   Coatsworth, p. 131-132.

2   John D. Martz, Editor, *United States Policy in Latin America: A Quarter Century of Crisis and Challenge, 1961-1986* (Lincoln, Nebraska and London, England: University of Nebraska Press, 1988), pp. 65-74.

3   Coatsworth, p. 137.

4   Shirley Christian, *Nicaragua: Revolution in the Family* (New York: Vintage, 1986), pp. 66-67. Robert Pastor, *Condemned to Repetition: The United States and Nicaragua* (Princeton University Press, 1987), pp. 66-71, 82.

5   Christian, p. 186; Coatsworth, p. 158: Pastor, p. 205.

6   Coatsworth, pp. 148-149.

7   Cynthia Arnson, *El Salvador: A Revolution Confronts the United States.* Washington, D.C.: Institute for Policy Studies, 1982, p. 45; Coatsworth, p.152.

8   Robert E. White, *"Weakness, Deceit and Consequences"*, speech delivered at the University of Texas, April17, 2008. Archived at http://www.ciponline.org/ central_america/WhiteSpeechApril08.doc

9   Ibid.

10   Ibid.

11   Blum, p. 357.

12   Jeff Cohen and Norman Solomon, "Jimmy Carter and Human Rights: Behind the Media Myth", *Media Beat,* (Fairness and Accuracy in Reporting), September 21, 1994.

13   Ibid.

14   Maziar Behrooz, "Surprise: Nobody Saw the Revolution Coming", *The Iranian,*

February 22, 2001. Though his administration continued support for the Shah's regime, Carter had personally advised the Shah to improve his policies concerning human rights. Said Carter to an interviewer: "When the Shah was in Washington for a state visit in November of 1977, his secret police, Savak, had fired into a crowd of peaceful demonstrators and killed, I believe, several hundred of them. When the Shah came to visit me, I took him aside into a small office that I had adjacent to the Oval Office, and I told him that I thought that he was making a serious mistake in violating the human rights of his own people through his secret police and in taking strong military action against peaceful demonstrators. I advised him strongly not to do this any further. He replied to me with some degree of scorn and said that not only the United States but all the European countries were making a serious mistake in permitting demonstrations of our people against our government, that this was obviously a communist plot to overthrow democracy and freedom in the Western world, and we were ignorant as leaders in not stamping out this kind of demonstration at its earliest stage. And he said that in the nation of Iran there were just a tiny handful of people who opposed his regime, and these were all communists, inspired and controlled from outside, that there was no indigenous threat to his popularity. That was his response. It was a very frank and fairly unpleasant confrontation, but in private." National Security Archive, "Interview with President Jimmy Carter", *Backyard: Episode 18,* Archived at http://www.gwu.edu/~nsarchiv/coldwar/interviews/episode-18/carter3.html

15 Cohen and Solomon, *Media Beat.*

16 John Pilger, "How Thatcher Gave Pol Pot a Hand," *New Statesman,* April 17, 2000. Archived at http://www.newstatesman.com/200004170017. Accessed on October 5, 2008. For a detailed examination of U.S. support for the Khmer Rouge, see Michael Haas, *Cambodia, Pol Pot, and the United States: The Faustian Pact* (New York: Praeger, 1991).

17 Itai Nartzizenfield Sneh. *The Future Almost Arrived: How Jimmy Carter Failed to Change U.S. Foreign Policy* (New York: Peter Lang Publishing, 2008), pp. 160-161.

18 Kathryn Sikkink, *Mixed Signals: U.S. Human Rights Policy and Latin America* (Ithaca: Cornell University Press, 2004), pp. 146-147.

Chapter 3

Bloodshed and Deceit

Domestic American Politics in 1980 and the Election of Ronald Reagan

However the policies of the Carter administration should be regarded there can be no question that the administration of Ronald Reagan was considerably more strident in its Central American policies. As with Carter, there is a considerable discrepancy between the claims of the administration and its actual behavior. Once again, the historical writing on this question is typically polarized on the basis of the ideological framework of the writer. William Blum summarizes the Reagan administrations' foreign policy towards El Salvador as follows:

The Reagan administration, to whom 'human rights' was a suspect term invented by leftists, had little fear of the too-soft label. Its approach to the conflict was threefold: (a) a sharp escalation...in the American military involvement in El Salvador; (b) a public relations campaign to put a human face on the military junta; (c) a concurrent exercise in news management to convince the American public and the world that the Salvadoran opposition had no legitimate cause for revolution; which was to say that what the Salvadorans had experienced during the previous two decades, indeed for half a century, had little or nothing to do with their uprising—this, it turned out, was the inspiration of..."left-wing terrorists" abetted by the Soviet Union, by Nicaragua, by Cuba." [1]

President Reagan himself indicated that these were indeed the policies of his administration, remarking that such policies were intended to "halt the infiltration into the Americas, by terrorists and by outside interference, and those who aren't just

49

aiming at El Salvador but, I think, are aiming at the whole of Central and possibly later South America and, I'm sure, eventually North America." [2]

Whatever the appropriate assessment of Carter administration policies towards El Salvador may be, there can be no denying that the "wild celebrations in the rich barrios" following the election of Ronald Reagan to the U.S. Presidency described by Ambassador White were justified from the perspective of the self-interest of the Salvadoran elite. President Reagan took office on January 20, 1981 after having won the Presidency by campaigning in part as a pro-military conservative and foreign policy hawk who would reverse the supposed weakness of the Carter administration in matters of relations with the Soviet Union and previous foreign policy "failures" in various Third World countries that the Reagan administration would come to describe as fronts in the Cold War. During the administration of President Carter, middle class Americans had experienced growing economic frustration resulting from rising inflation, escalating fuel costs, exorbitant interest rates and stagnation of real wages. While the overall standard of living for the "average American" remained quite high by historical or then-contemporary world standards, the phenomenal growth of the American economy during the post World War Two period and the resulting affluence had begun to settle. The growing economies of Western Europe and Japan had once again become competitive with the American economy.[3] Many Americans simplistically attributed these economic frustrations to the perceived ineptness of the Carter administration, and domestic American politics took a turn to the right in the 1980 election. Reagan's actual style of governing, particularly on social and fiscal issues, was much more "liberal" than his reputation. For instance, as Governor of California, he had signed legislation legalizing abortion and increasing the state's education budget, and America's national debt doubled during his presidency. These are not exactly stereotypical American "conservative" positions. Yet Reagan had also cultivated a conservative image for himself with tough talk against student radicals and black militants in California during his term as Governor along with his sharp denunciations of Communism, the welfare state and "big government." [4]

In the area of foreign policy as well, Ronald Reagan and his associates presented themselves as the antidote to the supposed decay of the 1970s. Reagan's worldview has been aptly summarized by the historian of U.S. foreign policy John Lewis Gaddis:

> Reagan relied more on instincts than on systematic study in shaping his positions: in this, he differed conspicuously from Carter. Derived from his Midwestern upbringing, his experiences in Hollywood, and an occasional tendency to conflate movies with reality, those instincts included an unshakeable belief in democracy and capitalism, an abhorrence of communism, an impatience with compromise in what he regarded as a contest between good and evil, and–very significantly–a deep fear that the Cold War might end in a nuclear holocaust, thereby confirming the Biblical prophecy of Armageddon. This was, to say the least, an unorthodox preparation for the presidency. [5]

At the time Reagan took office, more than fifty American military and diplomatic personnel had been held hostage for well over a year by Islamic militants in the American embassy in Tehran, Iran. Many ordinary Americans, ignorant of the history of the relationship between Iran and the United States, viewed this situation as a national outrage, blaming the Carter administration for the overthrow of America's ally, Shah Mohammed Reza Pahlavi, in 1979 by followers of the radical Shiite cleric Ayatollah Ruhollah Khomeini, and resenting Carter for his apparent inability to deal more firmly with the Iranians. The invasion of Afghanistan by the Soviet Union during Carter's administration likewise convinced many Americans of his supposed weakness with regards to waging the Cold War, or "fighting communism." Indeed, such myths surrounding the performance of the Carter administration on foreign policy issues persist to the present time. For example, the conservative newspaper columnist Charley Reese issued the following remarks concerning Carter upon the death of the Soviet dissident Alexander Solzhenitzyn in the summer of 2008:

> Solzhenitsyn's great mind and his complex thoughts can't be summarized easily, but he is certainly worth reading. His criticisms of our Western culture were valid. He never criticized the American people, but aimed at the elite who, at that time, were compromising with tyrants all over the place and spouting a materialistic philosophy. Jimmy Carter practically dismantled America's defenses, pardoned draft dodgers, betrayed American allies and seemed to embrace leftist guerrillas.[6]

Such was the perception of President Carter held by many in 1980. The reality was quite different. The United States military build-up that came into full fruition during the tenure of President Reagan was actually proposed and implemented in its initial stages during the Carter administration. Carter may have "pardoned draft dodgers" (Republican President Gerald Ford had earlier proposed a partial amnesty for draft resisters and military deserters during the Vietnam War) but reinstated compulsory Selective Service registration for young male Americans. As previously discussed, Carter's administration actually provided economic, diplomatic or military assistance to many "American allies" (anti-communist regimes with far right-wing governments as well as some left-wing but anti-Soviet movements such as the Khmer Rouge), including those whose "human rights" credentials were so unbelievably shabby as to seriously compromise the integrity of Carter's rhetoric and ostensible policy positions concerning such matters, the Salvadoran junta being among the foremost of these. [7]

The rhetoric and official statements of the incoming Reagan

administration promised a reversal of this supposed weakness in the face of America's enemies and a turn towards a hardline, confrontational approach in international affairs. The Reagan government was unquestionably more aggressive in its foreign policy ambitions than the Carter administration had been, although this was a matter of degree as opposed to polar opposites. Just as Carter had initiated a military build-up, so did Reagan escalate the build-up. Just as Carter had granted millions of dollars in military aid to the Salvadoran government during his final days in office, so did Reagan increase the amount of aid given to the Salvadorans. Just as Carter had turned on the revolutionary Sandinista government in Nicaragua after the Sandinistas had refused to be incorporated into the traditional client state system, so did the Reagan administration escalate hostilities with the Nicaraguans.

Reagan Administration Policy and the Salvadoran Civil War 1981-1983

With regards to Latin America in general and Central America in particular, the Reagan government moved towards developing closer relations with the military regimes that dominated the southern part of the Western hemisphere during the early 1980s. The corollary to this was an actively hostile stance towards movements or governments in Latin America that were pursuing social or economic reforms that were perceived as threats to U.S. interests. Central America was declared to be particularly vital to American defense and security needs, even more so than the rest of Latin America, the first time such a foreign policy distinction had been made in nearly sixty years. On January 24, 1982, President Reagan announced the Caribbean Basin Initiative, which promised economic aid and preferential trade and tariff policies to Central American and other Caribbean countries that undertook "market-oriented" economic reforms. Given the increased emphasis on the importance of Central America, nothing comparable was offered to other Latin American countries. Regarding each of the individual nations of

Central America, the Reagan administration aimed to overthrow the Sandinista government of Nicaragua, defeat the Salvadoran rebels forces through direct warfare, and encourage civilian rule in Honduras as the Carter administration had done, but also use Honduras as a base for the anti-Sandinista *contra* forces, for training the Salvadoran military and possibly as a base for American forces in the case of a future direct invasion of Nicaragua or El Salvador by the United States. An increase in aid to the military government of Guatemala was granted and substantial economic assistance was provided to the governments of Panama and Costa Rica in return for acquiescence concerning U.S. policy interests in the region.[8]

In the early months of the Reagan administration, El Salvador became the foremost foreign policy consideration so far as Central America was concerned. It was widely believed by many, including U.S. intelligence analysts, that a victory by the rebel forces seeking to overthrow the Salvadoran regime was imminent. The rebel forces of the FMLN-FDR had popular support against the overwhelmingly unpopular regime. The rebel alliance consisted of a coalition of five separate guerrilla groups (Farabundo Marti National Liberation Front) whose political arm was the Democratic Revolutionary Front, a coalition of centrist Christian Democrats, leftist Marxist radicals, Catholic clerics, dissident intellectuals and leaders of worker, peasant, student and professional organizations. The rebels had launched a so-called "final offensive" in January 1981, the very month President Reagan was inaugurated, with the hope of overturning the Salvadoran state. The offensive was not successful, but the rebel forces did prove themselves to be efficient and capable fighters despite the fact that the Salvadoran military possessed greater numbers of personnel and more powerful armaments. The Pentagon, at the prompting of Reagan's foreign policy staff, created a plan for the eventual destruction of the rebels. In 1980, the last year of the Carter administration, military aid to El Salvador had been $5.9 million. By 1984, the year of Reagan's election for a second term, the amount of aid peaked at $196.6

million and this was only military aid. Most economic aid granted to El Salvador by the United States under the cover of the Economic Support Funds was diverted to military purposes. ESF aid peaked at $285 million in 1985.[9]

The provision of aid to the Salvadoran government by the United States became a source of considerable conflict between the Reagan administration and the U.S. Congress. The known involvement of the Salvadoran military and the right-wing "death squads" with connections to the Salvadoran oligarchy in the perpetration of atrocities created an apprehension on the part of many Congressmen to continue to support the regime, particularly in the unconditional manner insisted upon by the Reagan administration. Congressional opponents of Reagan administration policy in El Salvador were typically inclined towards the view that the conflict there could not be effectively resolved simply through military defeat of the rebels without any efforts to address the causes of the civil war and argued that assistance to the Salvadoran regime should be contingent upon efforts by the regime at political and economic reform and curbing human rights abuses. Opponents also argued that a realistic settlement to the civil war would have to be the result of negotiations between the government and the rebel forces.[10]

The Perpetration of Atrocities by American Clients in El Salvador

"Now there is only the law of the jungle. There is no law." The oligarch pulled out a very large gun and placed it on the table. Pointing to it, he said, "Today in, El Salvador, this is the Constitution." Then he pulled out two loaded clips and placed them beside the gun. "These," he added, "are the amendments."[11]

That the Salvadoran military and paramilitary "death squads" operated without regard for ordinary humanitarian or ethical considerations in the course of carrying out repression in the period leading up to the Salvadoran civil war and during the course of the war is well beyond dispute. In 1981, the organization Human Rights Watch established a branch of itself, Americas Watch, for the specific purpose of monitoring the human rights situation in Central America. Americas Watch published an extensive report with regards to its findings and discoveries a decade later, as the war itself was winding down in 1991. This report by Americans Watch remains the most thorough and well-documented collection of information regarding human rights abuses during the course of the civil war, and directs its criticisms not only towards the Salvadoran government, armed forces and paramilitary groups but also towards the United States as well as the rebel guerrilla forces.

The primary targets of repression in El Salvador were literally any sort of groups or organizations that sought to challenge the political or economic status quo. These included opposition political parties, students or instructors from schools and universities, labor unions, peasants' organizations, community groups and officials and lay workers from the Catholic Church. This repression was not unique to the period of the civil war or the years leading up to the war but, as has been shown, was part of a cumulative process that contributed to the actual outbreak of the war. Additionally, thousands of Salvadoran citizens with no observable connection to dissident political activities were subject to arrest, murder, torture or disappearance. At the time of the report's release in 1991, not a single official of the Salvadoran government or military officer had been brought to trial for participation in such activities. Though such actions continued throughout the course of the civil war, incidents of this kind were most prevalent during the war's early years from 1980-1983. A slow but unsteady decline of such events followed in the war's subsequent years for various reasons.[12]

Specifically targeted victims of political murders numbered well into the thousands in the 1980-1983 period. As mentioned, such atrocities were perpetrated by two primary forces, the Salvadoran military itself and the right-wing paramilitary "death squads." Due in no small part to economic and military assistance from the United States, the size of the Salvadoran military quadrupled during the time of the war. Indeed, it was the Atlacatl Battalion, an elite combat force trained directly by the U.S., that was among the foremost perpetrators of atrocities within the ranks of the Salvadoran army. Virtually all units within the Salvadoran military were known to have participated in atrocities and most of the highest ranking military officials were personally linked to atrocities. The structure of the military itself was such that it was particularly resistant to external pressure to reform itself. Instead, the army functioned as fraternal organization of career military men bound by a code of silence so far as criminal or atrocious conduct was concerned. Enormous amounts of money given to the military by the Americans allowed the army the means by which to consolidate its own power and position itself beyond the reach of external control or criticism.[13]

It was the events surrounding the Salvadoran civil war that were largely responsible for the term "death squad" entering popular vocabulary. Such organizations operated in other parts of Latin America during the 1970s and 1980s, but it was in El Salvador where such lethal, extra-judicial, extra-legal units were most widely utilized by those seeking to eliminate political dissent. For a time during the early 1980s, the terms "death squad" and "El Salvador" became virtually synonymous to many people in the Western hemisphere. "Death squads" operated on a clandestine basis, with anonymous members, and using unmarked vehicles. The role of "death squads" was to abduct targeted individuals, interrogate them with the use of torture, and then murder their hapless victims. The bodies of victims were disposed of by leaving the remains of the deceased, usually mutilated and disfigured, on roadsides or among other victims in out of the way places. In 1982, 250 victims were found in a lava bed north of the capital city of San Salvador.

Death squads used a variety of tactics in order to instill terror in the Salvadoran population. Sometimes the victims would be gunned down in public areas or in broad daylight. Other methods of terror or intimidation included "publishing lists of future victims, sending their targets invitations to their own funerals, and delivering coffins to their doorsteps."[14] Paid advertisements in Salvadoran newspapers would threaten the murder of persons denounced as enemies of the state. Even very high-ranking officials were not immune to such threats. In one particularly brazen incident, a member of the Constituent Assembly was interrupted during a lecture to the elected body by a telephone call where the voice on the other end threatened to murder the assemblyman's family.[15]

The actual membership of these "death squads" was drawn from a variety of sources, including members of the regular military operating in an extra-legal capacity, private vigilantes recruited and organized by the wealthy and powerful, or individuals settling private disputes. Rarely, if ever, did the regular army or police make any efforts to curb the activities of the "death squads" during the time when the killings were at their peak. Indeed, sometimes uniformed soldiers and policemen carried out such atrocities themselves. Some of the death squads functioned on a totally anonymous basis while others adopted such names for themselves as the Secret Anticommunist Army, the White Hand and the Maximiliano Hernandez Martinez Anticommunist Brigade.[16]

As for the victims of the death squads, foremost among these were members of labor unions and peasant organizations. Under Salvadoran law, union organization, strikes and collective bargaining activities were restricted to private sector and small business employees only and illegal for agricultural workers under the domination of the plantation owners and employees of the Salvadoran state. Agricultural workers enjoyed no legal protections whatsoever and were essentially serfs to the large landowners who comprised the Salvadoran oligarchy. Even labor activity that was officially legal was effectively eliminated through extra-legal methods, such as murder and intimidation. Both American and Salvadoran officials would denounce union leaders and organizers as Communists with ties to the guerrillas irrespective of the actual political positions or activities of the unions. The actual number of labor and peasant organizers murdered by the military, the police and the death squads has never been precisely determined. Such killings were at their peak during the early years of the war, 1980-1983. Among the more egregious examples of such murders were the killings of forty workers for the Salvadoran Institute for Agricultural Transformation, an organization whose purpose was the establishment of land reform, during 1980 and 1981. The president of the Institute was assassinated along with two American employees of a U.S. financed organization aiding land reform efforts. The three persons were shot to death in a coffee shop by members of the Salvadoran National Guard.[17]

One Salvadoran labor organization, the Salvadoran Communal Council, experienced the murder of ninety-two of its members and associates by death squads, police, National Guard or members of the military during 1980-81. Eighteen striking factory workers were killed in October 1979 while seventy-eight others were arrested and tortured. Seven members of an agrarian cooperative were killed in November 1982. Three peasant leaders were abducted and tortured to death in November 1983. These incidents represent only a small sample of such occurrences, which were routine in El Salvador during the late 1970s and early 1980s.[18]

The persecution of Catholic clerics and lay workers who were involved in efforts at political and economic reform was the most widely publicized aspect of the repression sponsored by the Salvadoran political establishment during this time. As will be discussed in a later chapter, the Catholic Church had begun to champion the cause of the poor and disadvantaged in Latin American countries during the 1960s and 1970s. The Church began to play a central role in the self-organization efforts of workers, peasants and dissidents in El Salvador which in turn brought about the hostility of the government, the oligarchy and the military towards the Church. Among the most notorious incidents of religious persecution during the course of the civil war was the assassination of Archbishop Romero in 1980, the murder of three American nuns and another American, a lay worker, a short time later and the killing of six Jesuit priests in 1989. Eighteen priests and one Lutheran pastor were murdered between 1972 and 1991. Three relatives of one murdered priest, Father Jose Ernest Abrego, were also killed after they began to inquire into the circumstances surrounding his death. A popular slogan among members of the military and the right-wing paramilitaries was "Be patriotic, kill a priest." [19]

Politicians attempting to lead any sort of opposition to the oligarchy were assassinated. Those who survived fled El Salvador. Only extreme right-wing parties funded by the Salvadoran elite and a token opposition party, center-right Christian Democrats, were allowed to participate in elections with relative safety. Six leading members of the Democratic Revolutionary Front were killed in 1980. The leading opposition spokesman was abducted and strangled to death in 1983. The home of opposition leader Ruben Zamora was bombed in 1989. Even Christian Democrats were subject to such persecution. The Christian Democratic Attorney General Mario Zamora Rivas was assassinated in 1980 by masked gunmen. A Christian Democratic official of the Foreign Ministry was killed by a death squad. By 1983, thirty-three Christian Democratic mayors had been killed in Salvadoran towns. One town, El Carmen of the Cuscatlan province, experienced the murder of three consecutive mayors. A Christian Democratic member of the Constituent Assembly was abducted, strangled and shot in the head. Two rank and file party activists were abducted from a bus stop and killed.[20]

The media also became a target of the Salvadoran military and the death squads. Three dozen journalists were murdered during the course of the civil war. Media or journalistic outlets that criticized the Salvadoran government are subject to bombing and other violence by pro-government forces. The editor of the newspaper *El Independiente* was the target of three separate but unsuccessful assassination attempts.

The editor and a photographer from another paper, *La Cronica del Pueblo* were kidnapped and tortured to death in 1980. Four journalists from the Netherlands were ambushed and killed in 1982.[21] Students and education professionals were frequent participants in dissident political activities and were likewise frequent victims of repression, murder and torture.

The National University in El Salvador was closed from 1980-1984. According to data compiled by Amnesty International, ninety-six primary school teachers were murdered during 1980 and 156 teachers were killed in 1981. Thirteen university faculty members were killed in 1989. Most of these murders were carried out by members of the National Guard. An estimated forty students were killed during a strike in 1980. The leader of the National Teachers Union was assassinated in May, 1980. Two university professors "disappeared" in 1983. A teacher who was also a women's rights activist was kidnapped and murdered in April, 1989. Once again, these incidents are only examples of the violence inflicted on educators and students as a means of silencing opposition to the Salvadoran ruling class.[22]

Even health workers and human right monitors, both native Salvadorans and those from other countries, were targets of political violence. In November, 1989, five members of a community health committee were abducted and two were shot. A human rights worker, Roberto Castellanos, and his wife were murdered by the National Police in 1980. The offices of the Human Rights Commission were bombed by the National Police that same year. The organization's secretary was kidnapped and found shot dead. Numerous other human rights workers disappeared and were never located. Still others were arrested and tortured. A leading figure in an organization called Committee of Mothers and Families of the Detained, Disappeared and Assassinated of

El Salvador, Maria Teresa Tula, was abducted from a bus stop, raped and tortured in 1986.[23]

Atrocities committed against the general population of El Salvador by the military during the course of the civil war were extensive. Americas Watch observed that "the Salvadoran armed forces made little attempt to distinguish between the guerrillas and civilians residing in areas where the FMLN was thought to enjoy popular support and where its forces were active."[24] The Salvadoran army's war against the civilian population of the country was as brutal and extreme as its war against political dissidents. A general illustration of the army's tactics concerning civilian targets is provided by a particularly notorious incident that came to be known as the El Mozote Massacre.[25]

In December, 1981, the Salvadoran village of El Mozote was attacked by members of the Salvadoran armed forces. [26] An estimated 700 to 1,000 persons were killed, many of them children, women and elderly persons. Subsequent investigations would uncover the details of the killings, including "people hacked to death by machetes, many beheaded, a child thrown in the air and caught on a bayonet, an orgy of rapes of very young girls before they were killed" and a hesitant soldier who participated in the murders was told by his commander: "If we don't kill them (the children) now, they'll just grow up to be guerrillas."[27] On January 26, 1982, reports of this massacre appeared in both the international and domestic American press. Two days later, on January 28, 1982, President Reagan appeared before Congress and stated that the Salvadoran regime was "making a concerted and significant effort to comply with internationally recognized human rights" and "achieving substantial control over all elements of its own armed forces, so as to bring to an end the indiscriminate torture and murder of Salvadoran citizens by these forces."[28] This continued to be the official line of the Reagan administration throughout Reagan's term in office and was subsequently continued by the administration of George H. W. Bush.

El Salvador - A War by Proxy

In the early months of the Reagan administration the standard *modus operandi* was to maintain silence in the face of evidence of atrocities, deny that such atrocities had transpired or blame the guerrilla fighters of the resistance for any political violence that was taking place in El Salvador. During 1981, the first year of the Reagan administration a total of 2,644 killings of civilian noncombatants *in a single month* by the government, the armed forces and private paramilitaries allied with the government were documented by the Catholic archdiocese of El Salvador. Secretary of State Alexander Haig claimed the well-publicized killing of four American churchwomen was merely the result of collateral damage resulting from crossfire rather than deliberate murder. The U.S. ambassador to the United Nations, Jeane Kirkpatrick, made similar claims.

The Reagan administration's increased involvement in El Salvador alarmed many in the U.S. Congress. This escalating involvement was developing along a pattern similar to that followed by the United States in the early years of American intervention in Vietnam. In 1981, less than a decade had passed since America's disastrous involvement in Southeast Asia had ended. A substantial majority of both elected federal officials and the general American public opposed an escalation of hostilities in Central America and increased U.S. interference in the region, despite Ronald Reagan's landslide electoral victory over Jimmy Carter the previous year. Towards the end of 1981, the U.S. Congress enacted a requirement as part of a foreign aid bill that the administration of President Reagan issue documentation every six months that the Salvadoran regime was bringing its human rights policies up to international standards and transferring full political power away from the military towards civilian supervision. If the Salvadorans were to fail to comply with these requirements, military aid would no longer be given.[29]

The Reagan administration issued four separate certifications claiming the requirement imposed by Congress was being complied with until President Reagan finally vetoed renewal of the requirement in 1983. The Reagan administration altered its rhetoric concerning the human rights situation in El Salvador over time. Initially, charges of severe human rights violations were denied followed by gradual admission that some such abuses had occurred but denying their significance or claiming they were a thing of the past. The Reagan government would justify its positions by pointing to claims made by Salvadoran newspapers and by the Salvadoran military itself. This was in spite of the fact that the only newspapers allowed to function in El Salvador were those owned or funded by the Salvadoran oligarchy while independent or dissident papers were, at best, subject to either formal censorship or informal threats and, just as frequently, subject to bombings, kidnappings and the murder of journalists and editors. Claims by the Salvadoran army that individuals who had committed atrocities were being disciplined were taken by the Reagan administration at face value without efforts at verification. At the same time, the administration denounced and attacked the claims of human rights groups and relief agencies that had documented the repression and atrocities through such sources as survivor testimony or the testimony of eyewitnesses. Also, the administration denied that killings of "guerrilla supporters," whether actual combatants or not, were civilian massacres, instead claiming such incidents were part of the normal course of military action. This was a particularly astounding claim given that a primary strategy of the Salvadoran military was to undermine the guerrillas by targeting for elimination those sectors of Salvadoran society suspecting of sympathy for the guerrillas. As an illustration of this practice, the United States Embassy in El Salvador sent a cable to the State Department on January 25, 1984 stating that such casualties were "something other than innocent civilian bystanders" and described them as *masas*, a word used by the rebels to refer to their sympathizers among civilians, and characterizing them as simply "persons who live in close proximity of and travel in the company of armed guerrillas."[30] Implicit in this statement was the view that massacres of unarmed civilians, persons simply holding political sympathies more favorable to the rebels rather than the government, or residents of areas believed to be guerrilla hideouts or sources of civilian support were a legitimate military tactic, though massacres of this type are expressly forbidden by international treaties pertaining to the rules of war that the United States and El Salvador are signatory nations.

To what degree was the Reagan administration actually pressuring the Salvadoran regime for reform? Was the Reagan administration actually complicit in the atrocities committed by the Salvadoran armed forces and involved in efforts to obscure such atrocities? The most significant pieces of evidence that might help answer these questions originate from the more than 12,000 documents declassified by the Clinton administration following the end of the Salvadoran civil war and from the *Report of The Commission on the Truth for El Salvador* sponsored by the United Nations. Cliffard Krause of the *New York Times* reported that these documents indicated that "American officials knew far more about the workings of the military and the death squads in El Salvador than they told Congress or the American people." As an example, the American Embassy in El Salvador was in possession of refugee reports containing evidence of the El Mozote massacre while Reagan administration officials were denying the massacre had taken place. Ambassador Robert E. White had informed the State Department that the Salvadoran government was stalling the investigation of the murders of the four American churchwomen in 1980, yet Secretary of State Alexander Haig had proceeded to praise the Salvadoran regime for its efforts in the investigation. The Reagan administration also denied the involvement of ARENA party leader Roberto d'Aubuisson in the assassination of Archbishop Romero, yet the administration's Ambassador, Deane R. Hinton, had provided the administration with evidence of d'Aubuisson's involvement in the plot. At the same time President Reagan was proclaiming the U.S. client state in El Salvador was "achieving substantial control over all elements of its own armed forces, so as to bring to an end the indiscriminate torture and murder of Salvadoran citizens by these forces", a report prepared by the Pentagon and authored by Brigadier General Fred F. Woerner stated that

> "unabated terror from the right and continued tolerance of institutional violence could dangerously erode popular support to the point wherein the armed forces would be viewed not as the protector of society, but as an army of occupation." [31]

On March 26, 1994, the chairmen of the Senate Foreign Relations Committee, and the House Foreign Affairs Committee, and fifteen other members of Congress, sent a letter to President Bill Clinton asking for the declassification of U.S. government documents pertaining to human rights matters in El Salvador. President Clinton responded by directing the State and Defense departments, the CIA, and the National Security Council to release these documents. Persons involved with issues pertaining to El Salvador in the late 1970s and early 1980s have since offered varying assessments of the content of the declassified documents. Margaret Swedish of the Religious Task Force on Central America points out that the policies of the Carter, Reagan and, later, Bush administrations ran counter to both public opinion and the views of many in Congress. However, the Reagan administration was able to use its Central America policies as a means of enhancing its image as anti-communist "freedom fighters" in the eyes of some of its key constituent groups, such as the military and the so-called "religious right." Swedish also observed that much is missing from the declassified documents concerning the role of U.S. military advisers in actually conducting the war, remarking:

> People believe we had advisers in each of the garrisons and that there was a much more direct role being played by them in actually carrying out the war – I mean strategically planning with the Salvadoran army.
>
> Some of the military personnel down there, I'm sure, were

part of the intelligence agencies. This says little about the CIA role. That is a huge hole. We also have not seen much from the FBI and how they linked some of their domestic surveillance here with the El Salvador foreign policy. Another missing piece."[32]

Former Ambassador White suggested that "the State Department was perhaps the primary vehicle for the Central American policy and it's clear that lessons that should have been learned have not been learned" and that "unless we get the entire story out about what our actions have been like in Central America over the last four decades, the danger is that this will be repeated. Now I don't think it will be repeated immediately, but in 10 years? Who is to say?" [33] White made this statement in 1994, nine years before the present war in Iraq began.

Father William Callahan of the Quixote Center offered a far reaching analysis of the policies towards El Salvador and other Central American nations by successive U.S. administrations:

It was clear in El Salvador and was true in Nicaragua that the "solidarity folks," the U.S. church people, far from being the so-called naifs, have been absolutely right on target most of the time. We were lied to, cheated by the U.S. government. The bottom line is liberation theology's espousal of the poor. It was seen as a threat to U.S. strategic interests and to U.S. strategic allies. The (various administrations) didn't care how religiously based it might be, it stood in the way. They had to be marginalized. Since the days of the Banzer Plan of 1975, they've known what liberation theology was and what it claimed. They've known all along that Roman Catholics – many of whom were killed – were not communists in the sense of being loyal to Moscow, that type of thing. Yet in their determination that the so-called leftist element would in no sense be allowed to share power, human rights – even for Carter – were not in any way a U.S. priority that would be allowed to come into conflict with strategic interests. [34]

Bloodshed and Deceit

Cynthia Arnson was in charge of El Salvador for Human Rights Watch during the early 1980s. Arnson argued that a very important matter made public by the declassified material is that previous claims by U.S. policy makers that the atrocities and repression that transpired in El Salvador were not the responsibility of the actual Salvadoran government that was being supported by the U.S., but were simply the actions of extremists from the left or right, are shown to be false. Instead, argued Arnson, the Reagan and Bush administrations, "never told the Salvadoran government, 'You guys are thugs and murderers and if you don't clean up your act we're going to cut you off.' What they said instead was, 'These death squad murders are appalling and if they don't stop, Congress might do it regardless of our desire to keep on helping you. Congress might pull the rug out from under us.'"[35] Instead, the Reagan administration continued to arm and train the "thugs and murderers" at a cost of over a million dollars a day to the American public.

1   Blum, p. 357.

2   *New York Times*, March 7, 1981, p. 10

3   Don A. Rich, *"The American Empire is Another Bubble"*, Ludwig von Mises Institute, September 12, 2008. Archived at http://mises.org/story/3095. Accessed on October 6, 2008; Mark Thornton, "Skyscrapers and Business Cycles", *Journal of Austrian Economics*, vol. 8, no. 1, Spring, 2005.

4   Jeffrey Kahn, "Ronald Reagan launched his political career using the Berkeley campus as a target", *UC Berkeley News*, June 8, 2004.

5   Charley Reese, "A Giant is Dead", *Ottawa Herald*, August 11, 2008.

6   Gaddis, p. 350. Another example of Reagan's overly simplistic worldview is provided by Gaddis' description of Reagan's ideas concerned his Strategic Defense Initiative: "From an operational perspective, SDI was as remote from reality in 1983 as Khruschev's claims of strategic missile superiority had been in the 1950s. Reagan's interest in the concept had grown more out of incredulity that the United States lacked the means of defending itself against a Soviet attack and perhaps also out of movies and science fiction than from an informed assessment of what might be technologically feasible. Two decades later a workable system seems almost as far away as it did then." (p. 358) However, Reagan does not appear to have been the zealot for nuclear confrontation with the Soviet Union that many of his critics made him out to be. He remarked to Soviet Ambassador Anatoli Dobrynin: "Probably, people in the Soviet Union regard me as a crazy warmonger. But I don't want a war between us, because I know it would bring countless disasters. We should make a fresh start." (p. 359) Reagan also wrote that after watching The Day

El Salvador - A War by Proxy

After, a fictional film about a future nuclear holocaust that aired on network television in 1983, he subsequently met with the Pentagon top brass and was appalled to find that "there were still some people at the Pentagon who claimed a nuclear war was 'winnable.' I thought they were crazy. Worse, it appeared there were also Soviet generals who thought in terms of winning a nuclear war." (p. 360)

7	Cohen and Solomon, *Media Beat.*
8	Coatsworth, p. 164-165.
9	Coatsworth, p. 170
10	Coatsworth, p. 172
11	Tommie Sue Montgomery, *Revolution in El Salvador: Origins and Evolution* (Boulder, Colorado: Westview Press, 1982), p. 159.
12	*Americas Watch*, p. 17
13	*Americas Watch*, pp. 20-21
14	*Americas Watch*, p. 22
15	*Americas Watch*, p. 22
16	*Americas Watch*, pp. 22-23
17	*Americas Watch*, pp. 27-28
18	*Americas Watch*, p. 29
19	*Americas Watch*, p. 36
20	*Americas Watch*, pp. 37-39
21	*Americas Watch*, pp. 40-41
22	*Americas Watch*, pp. 41-43
23	*Americas Watch*, pp. 45-46
24	*Americas Watch*, p. 47
25	*Americas Watch*, p.49
26	Mark Danner, *The Massacre at El Mozote* (New York: Vintage Books, 1993).
27	Blum, p. 359.
28	Ibid.
29	*Americas Watch*, pp. 119-120
30	*Americas Watch*, p. 120-121, 53
31	Cliffard Krause, "How U.S. Actions Helped Hide Salvador Human Rights Abuses", *New York Times*, March 21, 1993.
32	Arthur Jones, "El Salvador Revisited: a Look at Declassified State Department Documents - Some of What U.S. Government Knew - and When It Knew It", *National Catholic Reporter*, September 23, 1994.
33	Ibid.
34	Ibid.
35	Ibid.

Chapter 4

The Resistance

The Salvadoran Opposition

Throughout its history, El Salvador had seen popular rebellions ever since the initial resistance to the *conquistadores* by the Pipil Indians in the 1520s. The earliest beginnings of the revolutionary struggle of the 1980s are usually traced to 1970, when the Popular Forces of Liberation (FPL), the first of the five guerrilla organizations that would comprise the FMLN, was formed. A second group, the Revolutionary Army of the People (ERP), emerged in 1972. Its membership was drawn from the outlawed Salvadoran Communist Party and the Young Communists from the radical Left, and also young people from the centrist Christian Democrats and politically radical members of the middle class. The leadership of both of these two early guerrilla groups was drawn heavily from religious circles. The ERP, in particular, included within its ranks many veterans of the radical movement that had developed within the Catholic Church in the 1960s. The ERP also included many Protestants, with two Baptist ministers being prominent among its leadership. The United Popular Action Front was formed in 1974 and drew much of its support from the *campesinos* of the Suchitoto area, who were being driven from their lands as part of the Salvadoran government's Cerron Dam project. Still another insurgent group was the Salvadoran Communist Party (PCS). While illegal since 1972, the PCS had taken a reformist political line and had worked through the electoral process by means of its above ground front group, the National Democratic Union. The PCS did not adopt a position of support for armed struggle until the February 28, 1977 massacres of citizens protesting electoral fraud at the Plaza Libertad. The Communists raised their own militias that were finally grouped together in 1979 under the umbrella of the Armed Forces of Liberation (FAL). The fifth group that would come to be part of the FMLN alliance was the Revolutionary

Party of Central American Workers (PRTC), which favored a transnational revolution across the Central American region. In October, 1979 these five groups joined together in an alliance under the banner of the Farabundo Marti National Liberation Front. [1]

Support for the insurgents was drawn heavily from the Christian Base Communities and popular organizations that emerged among the Salvadoran peasantry during the 1960s. These organizations had developed in opposition to the peasant organizations maintained by the government such as the Salvadoran Communal Union (UCS), which was funded in part by the American Institute for Free Labor Development (AIFLD). The purpose of these government organizations was to pacify peasant demands for better treatment and conditions by co-opting the upper strata of the peasant class and playing it off against the others as part of a "divide and conquer" strategy. The popular organizations and base communities were typically much more inclusive and democratic in their practices and organizational structures. Additional support for the insurgency was provided by the Popular Social Christian Movement (MPSC), which had emerged from the Christian Democratic Party as an opposition force to the party's leader, Jose Napoleon Duarte. Following the assassination of Archbishop Romero in the spring of 1980 an alliance of the center-left emerged that drew from the ranks of social-democratic political parties, small business associations, organizations of professional people and technical specialists, labor unions, academic and student organizations, and representatives of the Catholic Church. These groups then formed alliance with the political arm of the guerrilla forces, the Revolutionary Coordination of the Masses (CRM), and became the Democratic Revolutionary Front (FDR). From then on, the Salvadoran resistance forces would frequently be referred to in the international media as the FMLN-FDR. The former minister of agriculture, Enrique Alvarez Cordova, was elected president of the FDR, political offices for the alliance were established in Mexico with the permission of that country's government, and representatives of the FDR began touring Latin America and Europe with the hope of gaining international support for the resistance, an effort that proved somewhat successful. [2]

Two general strikes were held in the summer of 1980 in support of the resistance, one on June 24-25 another on August 13-15. These strikes involved the participation of workers, peasants and office employees, and ninety percent of the Salvadoran work force participated. The armed forces of the resistance were divided into the guerrillas, organized into squads and platoons and carrying out standard "hit and run" guerilla operations, and militias, composed of workers and peasants whose functions were to defend labor unions, towns and villages against government forces. These armed groups were supported by "popular neighborhood committees" which had the responsibility for collecting supplies such as food, medicine and weapons and engaging in logistical support for the insurgents.

The first major offensive by the FMLN began on January 10, 1981, an effort that was joined by a brigade of defectors from the Salvadoran army. After some initial gains, the insurgents began to retreat as the insurrection had been poorly planned and coordinated. The rebels would have suffered a greater defeat had not the performance of the Salvadoran military been even more inept. Meanwhile, the FDR political base in Mexico City began organizing not only political support for the resistance but also working groups of professionals and experts for the purpose of studying and developing solutions to El Salvador's many pressing political, social and economic problems. The group in Mexico City also took much of the responsibility for relief efforts necessitated by the huge wave of refugees and displaced persons generated by the war. This involved the full-time efforts of thousands of people beyond the rebel fighters themselves at a cost of millions of dollars on a yearly basis. [3]

Because of the small size and dense population of El Salvador, it was necessary that the guerrillas live and work among the common people, rather than camping out in the mountains as the Sandinistas in Nicaragua had frequently done. Instead, members of the FMLN forces would engage in farming activities with the peasants and provide medical care and self-defense training to local people. An underground network of supporters developed in the cities that procured essential goods, particularly medical supplies, that were provided to the insurgents. By mid-1981, it was estimated that the FMLN included 4,000 guerrillas, and 5,000 militia personnel. The principal problem faced by the rebels was a lack of armaments and arms that were outdated or difficult to continually supply with fresh ammunition. Throughout the course of the civil war in the 1980s, officials of the United States government, including President Reagan himself, repeatedly made extravagant claims about the amount of weapons being supplied to the FMLN by the Cuban and Nicaraguan governments and, by implication, the Soviet Union. Such claims were wildly exaggerated. Both the Nicaraguans and the Cubans had provided some level of military assistance to the Salvadoran rebels in the early months of the civil war. Such assistance was sharply curtailed following the lack of success of the insurrection of January, 1981. The Cubans were concerned about the effectiveness of the FMLN as a fighting force and, having experienced the disastrous results of Che Guevara's efforts to organize an insurrection in Bolivia some years earlier, had no desire for another quixotic adventure in another Latin American country. The Nicaraguans had initially hoped for peace with the U.S. and the eventual procurement of economic aid, and did not want to further exacerbate hostilities with the Americans. Some small amount of arms would continue to trickle into El Salvador from these countries throughout the course of the war. For instance, a plane coming from Nicaragua carrying anti-aircraft missiles crashed in El Salvador in November, 1989. However, most of the arms supply of the rebels came from purchases on the international arms market and from "corrupt" members of the Salvadoran military. The FMLN also learned how to make their own arms and set up weapons manufacturing centers in areas controlled by the guerrillas. Still more weapons were captured by means of direct engagement with the Salvadoran armed forces. An added irony is that the more the United States sent weapons to the Salvadoran military, the more weapons were captured by the rebels.[4]

Any examination of the Salvadoran resistance movement in the context of American foreign policy necessitates an evaluation of the ideological foundations of the resistance. This is an important matter given the rhetoric of American policy makers depicting the war as one where U.S. "national security" was being defended against Communist insurgents ostensibly aligned with or supported by the Soviet Union.

Historian Tommie Sue Montgomery says of this question:

By 1981 it was possible to discern the shape and character of the proposed revolutionary society in El Salvador from the organizations that already existed, from the forms of governance that operated in areas of the country under FMLN control, from the ideology of the revolution as manifested in everyday practice, and from the organizations' documents.[5]

During a press conference held on January 11, 1980, as the political alliance that came to be the FDR was being put together, the national flag of El Salvador was placed on the stage. One female speaker pointed to the flag and remarked, "The flag is not the property of the oligarchy. It is the only symbol of unity for us." [6] The press conference began with the national anthem of El Salvador. The following month a list of political objectives was published. These included bringing those responsible for the repression, the death squads and the murders and disappearances to justice according to standards outlined in the U.N. Declaration of Human Rights, devolution of political authority to municipalities, a neutralist foreign policy and expulsion of those tainted with the repression from the military. Banking, energy and commerce under the control of the oligarchy would be nationalized, but individual property holdings and small to medium sized business would be left under private ownership. There was also a call for tax reform, wider availability of credit, and the creation of public health, education and welfare systems. An additional document released on August 7, 1981 was read at the United Nations General Assembly by Nicaraguan President Daniel Ortega. This document stated that upon the achievement of peace by the resistance, those members of the armed forces not associated with the repression would be integrated into a new popular army along with members of the FMLN.

As the civil war progressed, the foundations of a new political system began to appear in areas controlled by the rebels. A concept known as "local popular power" emerged, with its core ideas being community self-management and "participatory democracy." [7] Periodic town meetings would assemble as the principal unit of government with an elected council presiding over such matters as health, defense, trade, and education in between meetings of the assemblies. The local revolutionary governments even created their own legal infrastructure and procedures for recording births, deaths, marriages and divorces. A sophisticated system of tunnels, modeled after similar works created by the Viet Cong during the Vietnam War, was established throughout the mountains of El Salvador. A campaign to provide milk to local children and to integrate traditional medicine with modern medical practice among local people and professional physicians was started, as was a literacy campaign.[8]

Women played an immensely important role in the Salvadoran resistance. At times peasant women would join the guerrillas merely as support personnel and subsequently become medics, armed combatants or even military and political leaders. Eventually, thirty percent of the FMLN's armed forces were female as were twenty percent of the guerrilla leadership. There were even all-female military units.

The presence of a wide divergence of political perspectives within the ranks of the resistance necessitated a fair amount of ideological flexibility. On one hand the movement drew heavily on both populism and nationalism, depicting the struggle as one against the domination of the country by the oligarchy and a government that operated as an American puppet. The strong presence of Christians, both Catholics and Protestants, in both leadership roles and among lay organizers, added a strong moralistic element to the resistance, one that viewed the struggle as one for peace and justice. The involvement of political factions ranging from Christian Democrats to Marxists necessitated a fair amount of political and ideological pluralism.[9]

The level of ideological pluralism and democratic practice that actually existed within the context of the Salvadoran resistance movement is particularly significant given the rhetoric of U.S. officials and the Salvadoran right-wing which depicted the resistance as a terrorist movement led by Communists. Ruben Zamora, a leader of the group of dissident Christian Democrats who eventually split with their party and formed the Popular Social Christian Movement (MPSC), argued that it was essential that the resistance be democratic and pluralistic in nature for several important reasons. One of these was the desire of the Salvadoran people for a democratic system, and the need to maintain a commitment to democracy in order to obtain and preserve popular support for the resistance. Another was to maintain open channels for self-criticism within the movement so as to avoid excessive bureaucratization and the resulting stagnation and inefficiency. It was also considered necessary for the resistance to take an inclusive approach to the varying social sectors of Salvadoran society so as to prevent these sectors from being co-opted or driven towards efforts by the United States to potentially gain control of the revolution if the rebels were to eventually achieve victory. Zamora remarked that, "At the present time, imperialism acts through sectors within the society; therefore, social sectors not incorporated into or neutralized by the revolution will fall into the hands of imperialism." [10]

The actual political program of the rebels more closely resembled objectives normally associated with social democracy than with hard-line Marxism-Leninism or Maoism, and there was an emphasis on participatory government, rooted to a large degree in the community organizations that came out of the radical wing of the Church and from lay Christian groups, that was arguably more democratic or "liberal" in practice than "liberal democracy" of the kind practiced in the Western countries. [11] A similar phenomenon had occurred in Nicaragua, where the revolutionary Sandinista government had eliminated the death penalty and limited all prison terms to a maximum of thirty years, a penal system considerably more lenient than found in many Western countries, and maintained a mostly private sector economy that was arguably less state-oriented than the American economy itself. [12] Indeed, the Nicaraguan Communist Party and a rival Maoist party operated as opposition parties during the time of Sandinista rule in Nicaragua, with the Communist Party itself eventually joining the pro-American UNO opposition coalition in 1990. A similar situation existed within the context of the Salvadoran resistance, with those holding pro-Soviet or reactionary Stalinist views finding themselves only on the fringes of the Salvadoran opposition.

The nature of the left-wing opposition in Central America was widely misunderstood in the United States. The efforts of American policy makers to depict themselves as champions of democracy and enlightenment in the face of benighted totalitarianism allegedly being advanced by the resistance movements were exceedingly obscurantist in nature. As the historian Greg Grandin observed:

The history of democracy in Latin American in the twentieth century offers a less pessimistic account of the relationship of the individual to mass movements. It was through political action most often associated with the left, including the Marxist left, that many of Latin America's most disenfranchised, from rural communities, plantations and factory floors, found a way to negotiate and physically stem, at least partially, the disruptions caused by capitalism. Rather than eliminating the boundaries between self and society, collective action distilled for many a more potent understanding of themselves as politically consequential individuals. Such insurgent individuality... was fundamentally necessary to the advancement of democracy, to the end of forced labor, and to the weakening of other forms of exploitation and domination.[13]

The Role of the Church

No discussion of the Salvadoran civil war can be complete without provision of an overview of the immensely important role played by the Church in the development of the poor peoples' movements of Latin America. It was the growth of these movements, and the efforts by authorities to repress or exterminate them, that were the real basis of the civil wars that raged in Central America during the 1980s. The growth of the Church-based radical movements of Latin America had their roots in Vatican II and the subsequent gathering of Latin American bishops in Medellin, Colombia. Traditionally, the Catholic Church in Latin America was very much a part of the "establishment" and constituted a branch of the ruling class "power structure" along with the landowners, business elites, military and government. The Second Vatican Council began in 1962 and continued for three years. The series of institutional reforms implemented by Vatican II included a greater emphasis on "social justice," or concern for the plight of the poor, along with the traditional religious concerns of the Church. The bishops gathered at Medellin in 1968. Penny Lernoux, a Catholic journalist who wrote extensively about the radical Church-based movements of Latin America, described the Medellin conference as "one of the major political events of the century: it shattered the centuries old alliance of Church, military and rich elites." [14] The alliance had extended all the way back to the original arrival of the *conquistadores*. Penny Lernoux described the movement that grew out of the Medellin conference as "the Magna Carta of today's persecuted, socially committed Church." [15]

These changes within the Church contributed to institutional division, as the ecclesiastical communities "Christian base communities" that grew up out of the application of the new teaching by lay people created conflict with the Church hierarchy. The hierarchy itself was also divided, with some Church officials expressing varying degrees of sympathy with the popular movements and others being vociferously opposed. The base communities operated on a relatively democratic basis, unlike the traditional Church hierarchy, and would elect lay preachers, and conduct Bible study among small groups. The Church hierarchy had traditionally taught that the common people should accept their position, and the oppression inflicted on them by the elites, and in return they would be rewarded in a future life. The theology of the new movements emphasized the role of God as the protector of the victims of evil or injustice drawing on, for instance, the biblical narrative of the Exodus of the Hebrew slaves from the tyrannical Egyptian pharaohs and Jesus' concern for those on the bottom layers of society as depicted in the Gospels.[16] This theological approach came to be known as "liberation theology," and it was this theological foundation that provided the inspiration for the ecclesiastical communities that emerged from the poor peoples' movement within the Church. "Liberation theology" was described by Tommie Sue Montgomery:

The reaction in the Latin American church to the conciliar and Medellin documents is usually described as falling into one of two categories, whether the reference is to the "historical" church versus the "institutional" church or to the "prophetic" church versus the "sacramental" church. The former term of each pair refers to the local church when it existed as small communities of believers without any bureaucratic superstructure; the latter refers to the institutional church with its bureaucratic interests that often have little to do with the fundamental values of Christianity, especially as they are interpreted by liberation theology. Whatever the labels, Medellin initiated a dynamic process of reflection that encourage Catholics (as well as Protestants) throughout the continent to rethink their faith. Most important, the emphasis on identifying the church with the poor led to the assumption of a more prophetic attitude towards politics and society. This has been expressed in a theology of liberation that has interpreted the gospel as demanding that Christians be a force actively working to liberate the great majority of the people from poverty and oppression. By the mid-1970s the theology of liberation had become the "common coin of discourse" among progressive Christians.[17]

The efforts by priests, nuns and lay leaders to organize the poor of El Salvador was met with repression and religious persecution on a level that was previously rare in Latin America. In early 1977, the pastor to the peasants of Apopo, Father Rutilio Grande, delivered a sermon where he expressed fears of the coming religious persecution. Said Father Grande:

I greatly fear that very soon the Bible and the Gospel will not be allowed within the confines of our country. Only the bindings will arrive, nothing else, because all of the pages are subversive – they are against sin. And if Jesus himself were to cross the border at Chalatenango, they would arrest him. They would take him to many courts and accuse him of being unconstitutional and subversive, a revolutionary, a foreign Jew, a concocter of strange and bizarre ideas contrary to democracy, that is to say, against the minority. They would crucify him again, because they prefer a Christ of the sacristy or the cemetery, a silent Christ with a muzzle on his mouth, a Christ made to our image and according to our selfish interests.[18]

A few weeks after delivering this sermon, Father Grande was assassinated, foreshadowing the assassination of Archbishop Romero three years later.

Romero's emergence as a champion of the lower classes of El Salvador and of human rights was initially a surprise to many who knew his background. He had a reputation for being non-controversial and a high-ranking cardinal at the Vatican had admitted that he was selected in part because the Vatican believed him to be a conservative who would avoid creating conflict between the Church and the Salvadoran government. Yet, the assassination of Grande and another priest, Alfonso Navarro, shortly before his installation as Archbishop increased Romero's commitment to speaking out against the regime. One of his first acts as Archbishop was to go to the then-President, Arturo Molina, and demand the release of another priest who had been arrested and tortured. President Molina remarked, "These priests of yours have become politicians, and I hold you responsible for their behavior," to which the Archbishop replied, "With all due respect, Mr. President, we take our orders from someone higher." [19]

Any effort to provide a comprehensive overview of U.S. foreign policy in El Salvador during the 1980s also necessitates some mention of the role of the Church in the United States. The U.S. Catholic Church and mainline Protestant denominations sharing the same concerns played an unprecedented part in organizing resistance to the foreign policy of the Reagan administration in El Salvador. The changes that had taken place in the Latin American Church since Vatican II and Medellin had also influenced American Catholicism and branches of mainline Methodism, Lutheranism, Quakerism and other Protestants. This fact proved to be puzzling to some observers, many of whom remembered the apologetics offered for the war in Vietnam by the likes of New York's Cardinal Spellman, and were used to the uncritical apologies offered for Reagan administration policy by the Religious Right. Awareness of the situation in El Salvador was also enhanced by the experience of American missionaries to that country. Three American missionaries were expelled from El Salvador in 1977. A right-wing terrorist group associated with the death squads, the White Warriors Union, made death threats against Jesuits, and other foreign religious workers in the country. The situation had become so severe that the U.S. Congress actually held hearings on religious persecution in El Salvador. Many U.S. Catholics, inspired by Pope John XXIII's efforts to address the severe social problems of the region had worked in Latin America during the 1970s. Protestant churches also maintained missions to Latin American countries during these years. These church people brought their knowledge of Latin America with them when they returned to the United States. The murder of the four church women in 1980 was a pivotal event for many U.S. people of faith, who were galvanized by their revulsion and outrage over the event.[20]

Many of these American Christians were at the center of the grassroots antiwar movement that developed in the United States in the 1980s. The largest U.S. antiwar groups included a substantial number of Catholics, mainline Protestants and members of other religious communities who opposed the wars in Central America. These organizations included the Pledge of Resistance, Witness for Peace, and Sanctuary. Sanctuary was a particularly significant movement, in that it involved the mobilization of nearly a hundred thousand Americans, the majority of them from religious communities, for the sake of providing safe haven for refugees from the wars whose flames were fanned by U.S. foreign policy. Many of these refugees were sheltered by Americans in direct defiance of U.S. immigration laws forbidding such assistance. These efforts helped to prevent to the return of unknown numbers of persons to countries where they faced likely arrest, torture or death. The U.S. antiwar movement also facilitated travel to Central America by thousands of U.S. citizens and helped to organize civil disobedience within the United States. [21] Christian Smith described how the U.S. antiwar movement functioned:

> Many of the movement's actions were isolated, relatively uncoordinated deeds of protest and solidarity. Handfuls of demonstrators in small towns held candlelight vigils

publicly to mourn El Salvador's war dead. U.S. cities "adopted" and supported individual Nicaraguan cities. Community groups shipped truckloads of clothing and tools to Guatemala's poor. Angry dissidents threw blood on the walls of government buildings. Community leaders wrote searing op-ed articles for local newspapers opposing aid to El Salvador. Ideologically directed consumers bought Nicaraguan-grown coffee in support of the Nicaraguan economy. Activist groups aggressively campaigned and voted against politicians who supported aid to the Guatemalan military. Middle-class citizens undertook hunger strikes and war-tax resistance. Outraged dissenters floated beach balls, painted to resemble explosive mines, in U.S. harbors to protest the mining of Nicaraguan harbors. Suburban homeowners planted in their front yards memorial crosses bearing names of individual peasants killed in Contra attacks. These kinds of grassroots expressions of activism reflected the movement's broad-based diversity and energy.[22]

The primary achievement of the extensively faith-based antiwar movement was to act as a constraining force on U.S. policy makers, thereby preventing the war against the lower classes of the Central American nations from becoming even more genocidal than it was. The principal achievement so far as actual policy matters was to pressure Congress to limit or reduce American military assistance to the government of El Salvador and other regimes or right-wing terrorist groups in Central America. Because of this pressure placed upon Congress, the Reagan administration resorted to funding the war effort by more covert and often illegal methods, a situation leading to the famed "Iran-Contra" scandal and near paralysis of the Reagan administration with regards to its Central America policy. Indeed, a number of major figures in the formulation of the administration's Central American policies were eventually brought up on criminal charges. Also, it is highly likely that the strength and activism of the antiwar movement prevented more direct U.S. involvement in Central America, such as a potential invasion of Nicaragua of the kind carried out against Grenada in 1983. [23] Yet the proxy war waged by American policy makers against the insurgency in El Salvador was still very costly to that nation, and ultimately began a war against the Salvadoran people themselves.

1   Tommie Sue Montgomery, *Revolution in El Salvador: From Civil Strife to Civil Peace* (Boulder, Colorado: Westview Press, 1995), pp. 101-105.

2   Montgomery, pp. 110-111.

3   Cynthia Arnson, *"Background Information on El Salvador and U.S. Military Assistance to Central America,"* Update no. 4, Institute for Policy Studies, Washington, D.C., April 1981 (memo); Bonner, p. 97; Alex Drehsler, "Revolution or Death!" *San Diego Union*, March 1, 1981; Montgomery, pp. 112-115.

4   Alex Drehsler, "Guerrillas Use Guns to Forge Marxist Society," *San Diego Union*, March 2, 1981; John Dinges, "Salvadoran Rebels Hold Base," *Washington Post*, January 22, 1982; Montgomery, pp. 116-118.

5   Montgomery, p. 118.

6   Charles Clements, *Witness to War: An American Doctor in El Salvador* (New York: Bantam, 1984), p. 123; Montgomery, p. 108.

7   Jenny Pearce, *Promised Land: Peasant Rebellion in Chalatenango, El Salvador* (London: Latin American Bureau, 1986); Montgomery, p. 120.

8   Montgomery, pp. 118-122.

9   Brenda Carter, et.al., *A Dream Compels Us: Voices of Salvadoran Women,* (Boston: South End Press, 1989); Montgomery, pp. 123-126.

10   Montgomery, p. 126.

11   Montgomery, p. 156.

12   Christian, pp. 167-168; Mary Ruwart, *Healing Our World* (Kalamazoo, Michigan: Sun Star Press, 1992), pp. 239-242. This is not to say there were no issues of repression in Nicaragua. Russell Means of the American Indian Movement discussed Sandinista oppression of the indigenous peoples of Nicaragua's Atlantic Coast regions in autobiography. Russell Means, Where White Men Fear to Tread (New York: St. Martin's Griffin, 1995), pp. 459-477.

13   Grandin, Greg. *The Last Colonial Massacre: Latin America in the Cold War* (Chicago and London: University of Chicago, 2004), p. 181.

14   Penny Lernoux, *Cry of the People* (New York: Doubleday, 1980), pp. 36-41.

15   Ibid., quoted in Bonner, p. 67.

16   Phillip Berryman, *The Religious Roots of Rebellion: Christians in Central*

America (Maryknoll, N.Y.: Orbis, 1984), pp. 104-106; Clements, p. 101; Pablo Galdamez, *Faith of a People: The Life of a Basic Christian Community in El Salvador* (Maryknoll, N.Y.: Orbis, 1986), pp. xvii-xviii; Montgomery, pp. 86-90.

17   Montgomery, p. 84.

18   Bonner, p. 65.

19   Montgomery, p. 93.

20   Dermit Keogh, Editor, *Central America: Human Rights and U.S. Foreign Policy* (Republic of Ireland: Cork University Press, 1985), pp. 1-5.

21   Christian Smith, *Resisting Reagan: The U.S. Central America Peace Movement* (Chicago and London: University of Chicago Press, 1996), pp. 59-61.

22   Smith, p. 59.

23   Smith, pp. 365-372.

Chapter 5

The USA vs the People of El Salvador

United States Foreign Policy and the Rhetoric of the Two Extremes

A persistent theme in the rhetoric of U.S. policy makers regarding El Salvador during both the Carter and Reagan administrations involved the concept of what might be called the "two extremes." Both administrations took the official line that it was the policy of the United States to assist in the establishment of a "moderate" and "democratic" government in El Salvador, with free elections, in opposition to the "extremes" of the Left or Right. The rebel forces of the FMLN guerrilla alliance and its FDR political arm were dismissed by the American government as mere "communist" or "left-wing extremist" insurgents committed to terrorism and the imposition of a Marxist state in El Salvador, with the likely subsequent effect of bringing El Salvador into the orbit of Soviet influence. At times, the rebel forces from the Left were even likened to the Khmer Rouge of Cambodia, and denounced as the "Pol Pot left" by American officials, even mavericks like Robert White.[1] It was an ironic claim given that these accusations leveled by American policy makers began during the same time that the United States was beginning to move closer to the actual Khmer Rouge, whose regime had been dislodged and its infamous "killing fields" revealed, as a possible ally against the Vietnamese and as a means of cultivating the Chinese as an ally against the Soviet Union.[2]

In a similar vein, the American policy makers consistently characterized the death squads, civilian massacres and acts of violent repression as originating from the "extreme right," which was said to exist independently of the alleged centrist, democratic government that the United States was supposedly trying to support against terrorists from both ends of the political spectrum. The Carter and Reagan administrations were both adamantly opposed to the resistance movement that sought to overthrow the Salvadoran oligarchy and military. Both administrations were fearful of a repeat of the 1979 Sandinista revolution in Nicaragua. The killing and repression carried out during the early 1980s was consistently blamed on renegade forces within the military or private right-wing terrorist groups operating illegally. The American government consistently sought to absolve the Salvadoran state itself or the Salvadoran military as an institution from responsibility for the atrocities.

The origins of the "two extremes" rhetoric of U.S. policy makers are traceable to the October 15, 1979 coup by a group of younger, reform-minded military officers who had hoped to implement genuine economic and social reforms, and to purge the armed forces of their most violent and out of control elements. While the coup was successful in ousting the previous Romero regime, the reformers quickly were overwhelmed by older, more experienced and politically-connected senior officers who quickly blocked efforts to implement internal reforms within the military. While willing to include centrists and leftists in the post-coup junta, even the reformers within the military were unsympathetic to the aims of the growing resistance movement. Instead, they regarded reform as a necessary means of preventing a revolution from the left. By January, 1980 all of the civilian members of the new government had resigned as it became clear the military's hold on the Salvadoran state would not be broken. The Carter administration might have been able to prevent escalation of the civil war if it had insisted that further American aid to the Salvadoran regime would only be forthcoming if the junta's promised land reforms were implemented, if the military was brought under civilian control and ended its repressive activities and if the United States had shown support for the comparatively "moderate" reform-oriented officers who had initially deposed Romero. While El Salvador was certainly an issue of concern to the Carter administration at this point, the situation in Nicaragua was the priority issue so far as Latin America was concerned, and the seizure of Americans as hostages in the U.S. embassy in Iran and the Soviet invasion of Afghanistan also transpired during these same months, and commanded much of the administration's attention.[3]

American policy towards El Salvador during this period was directed primarily by the National Security Council and the Pentagon. The leadership role in the formulation of policy largely belonged to Carter's hard-line anti-communist National Security Adviser, Zbigniew Brzezinski, whose primary concern was the prevention of left-wing influence in Central America. Carter himself was mostly preoccupied with the situations in Iran and Afghanistan. Rather than insisting on civilian rule or a purge of the armed forces, the United States, through deputy Secretary of State for Latin America James Cheek and the ambassador to El Salvador Frank Devine, brokered a deal whereby the military and the civilian Christian Democratic Party would agree to joint-rule. The Americans wanted the Christian Democrats in the government as a means of creating an appearance of moderation and civilian rule. This effort required considerable political maneuvering by the Americans and Ambassador Devine later remarked, "We were walking hip-deep through a swamp," and "It was like getting lions and tigers to forget each other's claws." [4]

Under the alliance between the Christian Democrats and the military, repression escalated to levels higher than it had been under the Romero regime that had been ousted by the October, 1979 coup. Even political assassinations of Christian Democratic officials themselves continued. There was a major split in the party over the decision to form an alliance with the military and many members left the party outright. Archbishop Romero asked the Christian Democrats to end any further collaboration with the military and he sent his famous letter to President Carter during this time. Carter did not respond directly. Instead, Secretary of State Cyrus Vance acted on his behalf, replying that

American aid was intended only to "enhance the professionalism of the armed forces so they can fulfill their essential role of maintaining order with a minimum of lethal force." [5]

Following the assassination of Archbishop Romero in March of 1980, both the American policy makers and the Salvadoran state began to fear that a revolution from the left was inevitable if not imminent. In order to defuse popular sympathy for the Left, a series of reforms were undertaken. These included a modest land reform program, and partial nationalization of the banking and export industries. The reforms did very little to improve the lives of the Salvadoran peasants, or to produce more equitable economic arrangements. The overall distribution of income continued to approximate what it had been prior to the implementation of the reforms, and there was no appreciable decrease in repression after the reforms had been put into place. The land reforms helped fuel the claims of the American government that it was helping a moderate regime maintain power in El Salvador in contrast to extremists from the Left and Right. The reality was that the army, police and death squads acted to violently eliminate those involved in implementation of the land reform, to the point of murdering employees of the Salvadoran government and agencies funded by the United States. The American and Salvadoran governments both repeated the claims that the land reforms were being attacked by the guerrillas, and this line was picked up by the American media and reported as truth. However, now declassified documents reveal that most of the violence against the efforts to carry out the land reform effort was the product of the Salvadoran right-wing, and sometimes even more conservative Christian Democrats. The American government knew this to be the case, but obscured this information in its official pronouncements. For instance, Richard V. Oulahan, director of the American Institute for Free Labor Development, circulated a memorandum in late 1980 claiming that seventy-two percent of the murders carried out in relation to the land reform program were committed by the army, police, death squads and "right-wing terrorist groups." The others were likely the responsibility of unidentified perpetrators originating from the same right-wing sources, ordinary criminals, or leftist guerrillas.

The Ideology of the Reagan Administration

Rivera y Damas was the Archbishop who replaced the assassinated Oscar Romero. After meeting with several top U.S. officials, including Vice-President George H. W. Bush, following Ronald Reagan's taking office, the Archbishop remarked:

> In light of my conversations, I am convinced that the administration does not understand the nature and composition of the junta. Specifically, I think you underestimate the power and resistance of the right-wing military to a true political change, including the kind of political dialogue which I am sure is the only road to peace in our country. When you and I discussed who the "extremes" were in El Salvador, I was surprised that you defined the junta as centrist and receiving attacks from both the right and the left which, to a certain extent, is true but what is more evident is the struggle between the junta and the left, aggravated by the fact that the high command of the military are principally members of the far right.

> Therefore your views of the junta as "centrist" do not concur with the reality and practice of the junta which is greatly influenced by the right-wing of the military. Failure to grasp the views of this element of the military, their power in the junta, and their resistance to change will be a fatal mistake for U.S. policy.[6]

Though this observation by the Archbishop accurately describes the rhetoric of both the Carter and Reagan administrations, it would only be a partial exaggeration to claim that when compared to the Reagan administration itself, certain elements of the Salvadoran regime were indeed moderate or "centrist," relatively speaking. As Raymond Bonner of the *New York Times* observed:

The Christian Democratic Party in El Salvador was far more liberal than Reagan's Republican Party; expropriating farms and nationalizing banks would not be included in any Republican Party platform and ran counter to the American party's emphasis on free enterprise. Rather than stress its support for (junta leader Jose Napoleon) Duarte and his party, the Reagan administration distanced itself from them. When Duarte visited the United States in the fall of 1981, he was not extended the reception frequently accorded leaders from even the most insignificant countries. He spent twenty minutes chatting with Reagan, thirty minutes with Bush—"and that was it," Duarte recalled. It was not an official state visit; there was no White House dinner, not even a joint press conference.

These slights were strong messages to the right and to the military in El Salvador.[7]

The Reagan administration regarded El Salvador as what might be considered a "test market" for its program of asserting American "resolve" and overcoming what the administration's key players felt was a decline of American power and prestige following the defeat of the United States in Vietnam less than a decade earlier, and the alleged impotence of the United States in the face of Iranian hostage crisis, the Soviet invasion of Afghanistan, and the overthrow of Somoza by the Sandinistas in Nicaragua. White House Press Secretary James Brady declared that El Salvador would be a means by which the U.S. would "send a message to Moscow." [8] Secretary of State Alexander Haig stated that El Salvador would be the place to "draw the line" in a renewal of Cold War hostility with the Soviet Union.[9] The Republican Chairman of the Senate Foreign Relations Committee, Charles Percy, echoed this sentiment, saying, "Haig is right, this is the place to draw the line."[10] The Assistant Secretary of State for Latin America Thomas Enders insisted, "There is no mistaking that the decisive battle for Central America is under way in El Salvador. If, after

Nicaragua, El Salvador is captured by a violent minority, who in Central American would not live in fear? How long would it be before major U.S. strategic interests-the canal, sea lanes, oil supplies-were at risk?"[11] President Reagan himself stated, "We believe that the government of El Salvador is on the front line in a battle that is really aimed at the very heart of the Western Hemisphere, and eventually us."[12] Such rhetoric implied, and often stated outright, that the insurgents in El Salvador were simply proxies for the Nicaraguans and Cubans, with these countries in turn being proxies of the Soviet Union.

From the start, such claims were wildly exaggerated and often completely fictitious. A high-ranking intelligence official under President Carter had stated that the FMLN was receiving nothing more than a trickle of firearms, ammunition or medical supplies from the Nicaraguans. Most of the FMLN weapons were stolen from the military, purchased on the international black market or captured in combat with the Salvadoran army. Former U.S. Ambassador to Nicaragua Lawrence Pezzullo revealed that a supposed boat landing in El Salvador carrying Nicaraguan arms was staged, probably a hoax implemented by the American Central Intelligence Agency.[13]

Reagan administration officials claimed that the "vital interests" of the United States were at stake in El Salvador. Yet the Assistant Secretary of State for Latin America under President Gerald Ford, Charles Bray, maintained that "the United States has no strategic interests in El Salvador."[14] President Ford's former Ambassador to El Salvador Ignacio Lozano testified before Congress that "the United States really has no vital interest in the country." [15] A former Foreign Service officer from the Eisenhower administration testified, "With the advent of the ICBM and Yankee-class submarines off our coast, how the hell can you talk about strategic interests? And all of that business that the traffic coming through the Caribbean is so vital to our interests – the fact of the matter is you've got Cuba in the Caribbean for the last twenty years. They could have intercepted those lanes anytime. You didn't need Nicaragua. You don't need the airfield in Grenada. This is just hyperbole." [16]

A notable characteristic of the Reagan administration's approach to policy concerning Central America was its total lack of interest in appointing persons who were genuinely experienced in areas involving Latin American politics. Instead, key positions were filled with ideologues often possessing dubious credentials concerning their suitability for such posts. This situation had its roots in the so-called "New Right" activist circles that latched onto Reagan's 1980 campaign. Greg Grandin described the process that transpired:

Months before Reagan's November 1980 election, would-be policy makers organized the ad hoc Committee of Santa Fe-one of the many groups formed by conservative activists in the 1970s to deal with foreign policy issues, this one specifically related to Latin America, to produce the document "A New Inter-American Policy for the Eighties,"...a classic example of New Right rhetorical action. It sounds familiar themes of Soviet expansion, American weakness, and looming ideological and moral conflict calculated to raise alarm and steel will...

Once in office, Reagan came down hard on Central America, in effect letting his administration's most committed militarists set and execute policy. In El Salvador, over the course of a decade, they provided more than a million dollars a day to fund a lethal counterinsurgency campaign. In Nicaragua, they patronized the Contras, a brutal insurgency led by discredited remnants of the deposed dictator's National Guard designed to roll back the Sandinista revolution. In Guatemala, they pressed to re-establish military aid to an army that was in the middle of committing genocide...All told, U.S. allies in Central America during Reagan's two terms killed over 300,000 people, tortured hundreds of thousands, and drove millions into exile.[17]

The Assistant Secretary of State for Inter-American Affairs was Thomas Enders, who had no previous experience with Latin America and did not speak Spanish. Enders had served in Cambodia during the Nixon administration and had been involved in selecting civilian targets for bombing, and obscuring atrocities perpetrated by the American aerial bombardment of Cambodia, in part through passing fraudulent information to the press and to the U.S. Congress. The Deputy Secretary of State for Central America was Craig Johnstone, who had previously been involved in the infamous "rural pacification" program in Vietnam. The head of the State Department's human rights division was Elliot Abrams, son-in-law of the neoconservative magazine editor Norman Podhoretz. Abrams quickly muted the department's criticisms of human rights situations in nations considered friendly to the ambitions of U.S. foreign policy. Bruce McColm was the administration's appointee to the Inter-American Commission on Human Rights. At the time, McColm had only published one "scholarly" work in his entire career: an exploration of the careers of retired rock stars.

The Ambassador to Nicaragua was Anthony Quainton, who was likewise ignorant of the Spanish language and had no diplomatic experience in Latin America. The new Ambassador to Mexico was an actor, John Gavin, whose only previous experience in that country was selling Bacardi rum in Mexican television commercials. The Ambassador to Honduras was John Negroponte, formerly a member of the National Security Council, who had criticized the Nixon administration for being "too soft" in Vietnam, even at the height of the Cambodian bombing. Lastly, the new Ambassador to El Salvador was Deane Hinton who, at age sixty, devoted the bulk of his attention during his post in that country to a romantic relationship with the thirty-year-old daughter of one of El Salvador's notorious "Fourteen Families," the oligarchs who controlled the Salvadoran economy, state and army. [18]

It was this rather unimpressive collection of characters that would formulate much of America's foreign policy towards El

Salvador, and towards Central America in general, during the early years of the Reagan presidency. One of the most influential Reagan appointees was the new United Nations Ambassador Jeanne Kirkpatrick, whose activities in that position included, among other things, pushing for U.N. recognition of the recently ousted Pol Pot regime as the legitimate government of Cambodia. In 1979, Kirkpatrick, then a professor at Georgetown University, had published an essay in Norman Podhoretz's *Commentary* titled "Dictatorships and Double Standards," where she argued against an emphasis on human rights as an aspect of American foreign policy, particularly when such considerations involved criticisms of states allied with the U.S. A significant part of Kirkpatrick's argument drew on the dichotomy she made between "moderately repressive" or "authoritarian" regimes, such as that of the deposed Shah of Iran or the Latin American dictatorships, and "totalitarian" ones, primarily meaning those of a "communist" (or anti-American) nature. The former were amenable to reform, she argued, and therefore deserved support from the United States. [19] Pat Derien, a former official in Carter's State Department, ridiculed Kirkpatrick's views saying, "What the hell is 'moderately repressive' – that you only torture half of the people, that you only do summary executions now and then?" [20]

On February 23, 1981, a so-called "white paper," called "Communist Interference in El Salvador," emerged. [21] In this document, the Reagan administration claimed it had definitive proof that the Salvadoran guerrillas were fighting to overthrow the government of El Salvador on behalf of Cuba and the Soviet Union.[22] The claims of the white paper were thoroughly debunked by those journalists who made the effort to verify them, but most journalists did not do this. Instead, the administration's claims were widely circulated as fact within the mainstream American media. [23] The white paper cited documents supposedly captured from the FMLN that indicated Soviet involvement with the insurgency. These documents were later exposed as forgeries. Still other documents were deliberately mistranslated from the original Spanish to conform to what the administration wanted the American public to believe concerning the situation in El Salvador. Indeed, some of the documents directly contradicted the claims of the administration. As an example, an official of the Salvadoran Communist Party had traveled to Moscow seeking aid for the insurgency, only to be given a cold reception and failing to secure a commitment from the Soviets for assistance. The documents also indicated the guerrillas suffered from a chronic shortage of weapons, and that the neighboring Nicaraguans had objected to FMLN attempts at weapons smuggling through their own country.[24] The Reagan administration also claimed that the 10,000 murders perpetrated by the Salvadoran military and "death squads" during 1980 were mostly fictitious and the product of "leftist propaganda" even though the actual statistics were drawn from reports compiled by Amnesty International, Americas Watch, and the U.S. embassy in San Salvador itself. The senior U.S. diplomat to Cuba between 1979 and 1982, Wayne Smith, later confirmed, "We never had solid evidence of massive and substantial flow of arms from Cuba to Nicaragua and then to El Salvador." [25]

The Reagan's Administration's Proxy War and the Impact of Reagan Administration Policies in the Continuation of the Salvadoran Civil War

When members of the U.S. Congress, the American media or the general American public would express concern about the similarities between American involvement in Central America in the 1980s and previous involvement in Vietnam in the 1960s, the Reagan administration would attempt to counter such objections by insisting that its efforts in Central America were for the purpose of *preventing* the escalation of the wars in the region to the level previously observed in Southeast Asia. Administration apologists would claim that "communism" needed to be defeated early in the struggle for Central America, so that it would not be necessary to wage a much larger war at some point in the future with "communist" dominated Central American nations operating as satellites for the Soviet Union in the same manner as the Warsaw Pact countries of Eastern Europe. In other words, the rationale advanced by the Reagan administration for its policies in El Salvador, Nicaragua, Guatemala and Honduras was that support for the governments of those countries (or, in the case of Nicaragua, the *contra* guerrilla forces) would help to defeat "communism" in the short run, thereby preventing a larger war with the full-scale use of American forces in the long-run.

While the arguments against these claims were numerous and substantive, the fact that these arguments were advanced by the administration makes it clear that American policy makers regarded the recipients of American assistance in the wars in Central America, including the government of El Salvador, as proxy forces, that is to say, as forces who were being used by the Reagan administration for the purpose of obtaining its own foreign policy objectives. The government of El Salvador, for instance, enjoyed very little popular support, and military analysts believed its eventual overthrow by the rebel forces was highly probable. The American government became the benefactor of the Salvadoran state, with the Salvadorans in turn becoming instruments of American foreign policy.

The amount of money spent by the American government on keeping the Salvadoran regime in power increased exponentially with the passing of each fiscal year. Much of this was done without even the approval of the U.S. Congress. The power of the executive branch of government under the Foreign Assistance Act to provide immediate military assistance in emergency situations was invoked and funds provided by Congress for aid to other countries would be shifted to El Salvador. The administration also pushed international agencies such as the World Bank, International Monetary Fund and the Inter-American Development Bank, along with other transnational banking entities, to provide exorbitant loans or grants to the government of El Salvador, which would then be used on the war effort. The Salvadoran regime received $111 million dollars from such sources in the years between 1981-1983 alone.[26]

Formally, the Reagan administration limited the actual number of U.S. military advisors in El Salvador to fifty-five, the maximum number allowed by Congress. However, more than a hundred advisors were sent to Honduras to train Salvadoran troops inside that country. Still another twenty-six advisors were sent whom the administration claimed were "medics." These were, in fact, members of the U.S. Special Forces who simply had prior training as medics. The U.S. also constructed a multi-million dollar military base in Honduras, with 1,040 Salvadoran troops being stationed there to obtain training from the Americans. The notorious Atlacatl battalion was trained at the American base in Honduras. Five hundred Salvadoran troops were trained as officers at the infamous School of the Americas at Fort Benning, Georgia and a Salvadoran battalion also received training at Fort Bragg, North Carolina.[27]

During the first three years of the Reagan presidency, the size of the Salvadoran armed forces tripled to more than twice the size of the Nicaraguan army which the administration claimed to be so formidable. Still, the Salvadoran regime was not able to defeat the insurgency due to the lack of popular support for itself and the extraordinarily inept performance of the Salvadoran forces. Even many U.S. officials expressed disgust and frustration with the failures of the Salvadoran army. Officers in the Salvadoran army were unaccustomed to genuine combat and were more experienced at carrying out repression against usually unarmed civilians. The officers would deliberately avoid danger to themselves, and most of the casualties were rank and file troops, many of them in their early teens, who had been pressed into military service during raids on villages and youth "hang outs" such as theaters. The U.S. policy makers continued to escalate the war with American planes based in Panama conducting surveillance flights over El Salvador. Direct military involvement in El Salvador by U.S. forces continued to be avoided by acting indirectly through Honduras instead. The amount of U.S. military aid to Honduras for the single year of 1982 was roughly equal to that of the previous thirty-five years combined. The amount of internal repression in Honduras began to grow and at times resembled that of El Salvador. It is also known that mercenaries, many of them with combat experience in Vietnam, were employed through the Central Intelligence Agency for operations in El Salvador, though the precise scale of this project is difficult to determine. A consequence of the Reagan administration's provision of massive assistance to the Salvadoran regime is that the civil war continued for a much longer period than what it would have been if American aid had been withheld. Additionally, the Reagan administration was adamantly opposed to a negotiated settlement with the resistance. Under no conditions were the guerrillas to be allowed to participate in governing El Salvador. Yet the continuing rule of the junta representing the Christian Democratic-military coalition generated much criticism concerning the administration policy in El Salvador, and so the administration sought to mute such criticism by creating a veneer of civilian or democratic rule.[28]

Ballots and Bullets

The U.S. policy makers formulated a plan for a series of elections, which the Salvadoran junta announced in March of 1981. These were scheduled to be held over the next several years. Edward S. Herman and Frank Broadhead referred to these as "demonstration elections," whose intention was "to convince the citizens of the United States that their client government is freely chosen" and to "ratify political leaders chosen by the (Reagan) administration." [29] The conditions in El Salvador were not conducive to the holding of elections by any reasonable standard of legitimacy. The media at the time was subject to severe censorship. Popular political organizations had either disbanded or gone underground, and a state of emergency had been in effect for over two years when the first elections were held. Open death threats and promises of assassination had been made against opposition leaders, and violent repression continued to be the norm. By 1982, over 30,000 people had been killed through war and repression and another 500,000 refugees had been produced. Citizens were required by law to vote. Failure to do so was considered treason, with the identity cards of voters being stamped in a way that indicated whom an individual had voted for.[30]

The contending parties for the 1982 elections were the extreme right-wing Nationalist Republican Alliance (ARENA) led by the fascist Roberto D'Aubuisson, who had been encouraged to form a party of his own by various forces from the American Right, who provided assistance to ARENA's campaign efforts. [31] The "Republican" part of the party's name was an expression of appreciation to the U.S. Republican Party. Another party was the Christian Democrats of junta president Jose Napoleon Duarte, which had lost more than sixty percent of its members, many of whom had joined the insurgency, as Duarte's entering an alliance with the military was considered a betrayal. The other two parties were the Party of National Conciliation and Democratic Action Party, with the former viewing itself as a force for greater unity between the Christian Democrats and the military, and the latter representing the class of lawyers that served the oligarchy. The social democratic MNR and the MPSC, a party of dissident Christian Democrats, were asked to participate, but refused, given the violent conditions in El Salvador. More than sixty local mayors representing these parties had already been killed by death squads. The remaining leaders were in exile in Mexico or other nations, and were told they would be allowed to campaign by television. This offer was refused, as the FDR was not allowed to participate, and the MNR and MPSC viewed this as a means of dividing the opposition. Representatives of the FMLN were also forbidden to participate, though their leaders had made numerous offers for open negotiations for the purpose of ending the civil war. The individual commanders of the five groups comprising the FMLN had even sent a letter stating their positions regarding negotiations to President Reagan.[32]

The Defense Department, CIA and other organizations representing the U.S. government provided unknown amounts of funds for the election. The campaign itself was essentially a rivalry between Duarte and D'Aubuisson, with the latter's campaign slogan being "Tremble, Tremble, Communists." Though he had the support of certain right-wing Republican elements in the United States, the Reagan administration itself feared a victory by D'Aubuisson would undermine the public relations purposes for which the U.S. was holding the election and pushed for a Duarte victory instead. The election itself was conducted haphazardly, with voters often having to walk for miles to reach a limited number of polling places, often under the watch of the army, and with twenty-eight separate localities under control by the guerrillas effectively preventing much of the rural population from participating. Duarte's Christian Democrats actually received more votes than the other parties, but together the three extreme right-wing parties won enough seats to collectively dominate the new Assembly, and D'Aubuisson was named the Assembly's new president.

As the war continued to rage and the numbers of casualties, refugees and human rights violations continued to escalate. [33] Pope John Paul II visited El Salvador, paid tribute to the assassinated Archbishop Romero, and called for peace through a negotiated settlement to the war, encouraging then Archbishop Rivera Damas to act as a mediator.

The methods used in the conduct of the war by the Salvadoran military, and the U.S. administration's support for the regime, increasingly became a source of international outrage, and to such a degree that the administration began making stronger efforts to at least give the appearance of trying to control the death squads. Ambassador Deane Hinton was replaced by Thomas Pickering, who gave a speech denouncing the death squads. A promise, of dubious sincerity, to curb death squad activity was solicited from the Salvadoran Defense Minister. Roberto D'Aubuisson was denied a visa to enter the United States. A number of high ranking American officials paid personal visits to El Salvador, including Elliot Abrams and Vice-President George H. W. Bush, who personally delivered a letter from President Reagan to the military's handpicked president, Alvaro Magana. The letter from Reagan identified a number of governmental and military officials believed to be associated with the death squads and insisted that these individuals be removed from their positions, or U.S. military aid might be terminated or suspended. Reagan also personally contacted Magana by telephone requesting the investigation and prosecution of a Salvadoran army lieutenant accused of murdering two Americans employed by U.S. government-financed agencies involved with land reform projects in El Salvador.[34] The Salvadorans failed to dismiss or prosecute anyone accused by the United States of involvement with the death squads, but U.S. military aid not only continued but increased, and Reagan vetoed legislation extending the requirement that the administration issue a report to Congress every six months demonstrating reasonable progress in improving the human rights situation in El Salvador. However, the added pressure from the Americans, while miniscule, had some tangible effect as the number of persons killed or missing dropped substantially in 1984.

Another U.S. financed election was held in 1984, this one being conducted as haphazardly as the previous one, with many reports of vote buying and other forms of corruption. The areas of El Salvador under FMLN control now numbered forty two localities rather than the twenty-eight from two years earlier. The U.S. once again feared a public relations disaster if D'Aubuisson emerged victorious, and so the CIA poured money into the Christian Democrats' campaign, thereby helping to elect Jose Napoleon Duarte.[35] The worst years of the war had now passed, but the achievement of peace was still years away.

1   Bonner, p. 184.

2   Blum, p. 139.

3   Bonner, pp. 159-164.

4   Bonner, p. 167.

5   Bonner, pp. 171-173.

6   Bonner, pp. 200-201.

7   Bonner, p. 230.

8   Bonner, p. 231; Jose Napolean Duarte with Diana Page, *Duarte: My Story* (New York: G.P. Putnam's Sons, 1986), pp. 157-176.

9   Bonner, p. 233.

10   Ibid.

11   Ibid.

12   Bonner, p. 234.

13   Ibid.

14   Bonner, pp. 227-228.

15   Bonner, pp. 234-235.

16   Ibid.

17   Ibid.

18   Greg Grandin, *Empire's Workshop: Latin America, The United States, and the Rise of the New Imperialism* (New York: Metropolitan Books, 2006), pp. 69-71.

19   Bonner, pp. 244-253. An amusing anecdote concerning Hinton involved the fact that while he was the American ambassador to El Salvador, he sent a birthday check to his daughter in London, which she promptly donated to a FMLN solidarity group (Bonner, p. 253).

20   Bonner, pp. 236-237; Jeane J. Kirkpatrick, "Dictatorships and Double Standards", Commentary, November, 1979. Ironically, Kirkpatrick was one-time adherent of the radical Left. Joshua Muravchik of National Review describes a surreal and almost unbelievable event that transpired on "May Day" of 2002 in Washington, D.C.: "May Day passed quietly this year in Red Square where the rumble of mobile missile launchers and the beat of goose-stepping soldiers used to celebrate the power of the proletariat. But there was noise aplenty just off Dupont Circle in Washington, where upwards of a hundred aging one-time American Reds belted out beery refrains of 'Which Side Are You On?' and 'The Internationale.' These were Reds of a different hue. Not Communists. But former members of the Socialist Party — led once by Eugene Victor Debs and later Norman Thomas — and of its youth group, the Young People's Socialist League ("Yipsel"). This party never escaped the margins of American politics, but a fair number of its members — radicals of the '30s or '60s — eventually made their mark, some on the left, some on the right, and many of these convened this May Day for a kind of Socialist all-class reunion. Among those sponsoring or joining the evening's festivities — funded mainly by the estate of the widow of Trotskyist

icon Max Shachtman — were, on the right, former U.N. ambassador Jeane Kirkpatrick, former Christian Coalition spokesman Marshall Wittmann, and former Secretary of Labor nominee Linda Chavez; and, on the Left, teachers' union chief Sandra Feldman, Clinton USIA director Penn Kemble, and New Yorker editor Hendrik Hertzberg. In between were former arms negotiator Max Kampelman, National Endowment for Democracy President Carl Gershman, and scholars like Nathan Glazer and Seymour Martin Lipset." Joshua Muravchik, "Marx Meet Oedipus," National Review, May 8, 2002.

21   Bonner, p. 255. See also *The Report of the President's National Bipartisan Commission on Central America* (New York: Macmillan, 1984), Henry A. Kissinger, Chairman.

22   Bonner, p. 255. Such claims were not particularly original. A similar statement was made by the U.S. Secretary of State Frank Kellogg in the 1920s. Kellogg insisted the Mexican government of the time was conspiring with the Soviet Union and the Nicaraguans to bring "Bolshevik hegemony" to Central America. The core issues of the dispute were efforts by the Mexicans to obtain more control over American-owned oil companies operating in the Mexican nation. Ronald Steel, Walter Lippman and the American Century (Boston: Little and Brown, 1980), p. 237.

23   John Dinges, "White Paper or Blank Paper?" *Los Angeles Times*, March 17, 1981: James Petras, "White Paper on the White Paper," The Nation, March 28, 1981; Robert G. Kaiser, "White Paper on El Salvador is Faulty," *Washington Post*, June 9, 1981; Jonathan Kwitney, "Apparent Errors Cloud U.S. 'White Paper' on Reds in El Salvador, *Wall Street Journal*, June 8, 1981; Ralph McGehee, "The CIA and the White Paper on El Salvador," *The Nation*, April 11, 1981.

24   Bonner, pp. 256-260

25   Bonner, pp. 259.

26   Bonner, p. 271.

27   Bonner, pp. 277-278.

28   Bonner, pp. 279-284.

29   Frank Brodhead, "Demonstration Elections in El Salvador," in Marvin E. Gettleman, et. al., *El Salvador: Central America in the New Cold War*, rev. ed. (New York: Grove Press, 1986), p. 175. Edward S. Herman and Frank Brodhead, *Demonstration Election: U.S.-Staged Elections in the Dominican Republic, Vietnam and El Salvador* (Boston: South End Press, 1984).

30   Montgomery, p. 156-157.

31   Craig Pyes, "The New American Right Picks Up a Hot Potato," *Albuquerque Journal*, December 22, 1983, pp. A-1, A6-10.

32   Montgomery, p. 153, 158.

33   For a discussion of human rights issues concerning the FMLN, see Montgomery, pp. 118, 206-207. These issues include: kidnapping and ransoming of wealthy Salvadorans, summary executions of suspect collaborators with the army, mistreatment or killing of captured soldiers, killing of civilian passengers in vehicles that failed to stop at roadblocks,

political assassinations and assassinations of U.S. military personnel, forced recruitment, kidnappings of mayors and kidnapping the daughter of President Duarte, forced relocation of civilians in rebel-occupied territories, and the planting of mines. Still, the record of atrocities committed by the resistance pales in comparison to that of the government, the army and the death squads. Montgomery found that in her interviews of Salvadoran refugees in Belize, ninety percent left because of actions or fears induced by the army and security forces. The United Nations Truth Commission for El Salvador found that the army, security forces and death squads had been responsible for ninety-five percent of the human rights abuses in the civil war, and the FMLN responsible for the other five percent (Montgomery, p. 242).

34   Montgomery, pp. 177-178, Bonner, p. 45.

35   Montgomery, pp. 182-83.

Epilogue

The Duarte Years

Jose Napoleon Duarte had finally achieved his lifelong ambition of becoming President of El Salvador.[1] Duarte's victory in 1984 increased the standing of the Salvadoran regime among members of the U.S. Congress and Congress subsequently voted for hundreds of millions of dollars in additional military aid to the regime. Duarte's presidency was a serious failure on many levels. He failed to achieve control over the military and the army continued to be the *de facto* rulers of the country. When the FMLN-FDR offered to meet with Duarte for peace talks, he ignored their gesture for a full five months before agreeing to a meeting during a speech to the United Nations General Assembly. His primary efforts were directed at winning the favor of international opinion and placating the military. Though token steps were taken by Duarte to curb human rights abuses, no significant action was taken against those most directly responsible for the death squads of the previous years. Duarte's party was also a minority party in the legislature, a situation that paralyzed his efforts there.

Two separate meetings with representatives of the FMLN-FDR failed to produce any results. The resistance had offered a comprehensive peace plan, with Duarte in turn denouncing the rebels on television after the meeting. Duarte's complete rejection of the offer was likely done in part to satisfy the military, the oligarchy and possibly the Reagan administration, all of whom vigorously opposed the plan. His major economic policy was to devalue El Salvador's currency, the *colon*, an idea favored by the Americans for the sake of increasing exports and reducing imports. This policy had a disastrous effect on the Salvadoran economy and was strongly opposed by members of the Salvadoran oligarchy and workers' organizations alike, reaffirming the view of both the Right and the Left in El Salvador that Duarte was simply an

American puppet, installed by the Reagan administration's State Department and CIA for cosmetic purposes.[2]

The elections of 1982 and 1984 had the unintended consequence of galvanizing popular self-organization among Salvadorans of the kind that had disappeared with the escalation of repression and civil war. Labor unions had continued to organize on an underground basis during the repression and had once again started to engage in mass demonstrations and strikes during the Duarte period. The leadership of these newer organizations tended to be less ideologically rigid or extreme than some of their predecessors, and were consequently more adept at organizing and building stable political coalitions. The Christian Democrats went on to be the dominant party in the legislative elections of 1985. ARENA accused the Christian Democrats of fraud in the 1985 elections, and sought to nullify the results, but the army itself rejected ARENA's demands, an indication of a growing gap between the army as an institution and parties of the extreme right-wing. Even within ARENA, comparatively "moderate" forces began to assert themselves against D'Aubuisson's previously unchallenged leadership. Corruption within the Christian Democratic regime of Duarte continued unabated as it had under previous military governments, nor was there any serious effort at bringing perpetrators of the atrocities during the early 1980s to justice. The civil war continued with neither a stalemate nor a victory for either side in sight.

Several positive developments transpired by the end of the Duarte era. First, the growing "Iran-Contra" scandal in the United States weakened the ability of the American government to operate with a free hand in Central America as the Reagan administration's policies there became subject to increased scrutiny by the American public and American media. The President of Costa Rica, Oscar Arias, led an effort by the heads of state of the Central American nations to find a way to peace with regards to the various wars being waged in the region at the time. Duarte consequently felt pressure to negotiate with the resistance. The FMLN-FDR initially agreed to further talks with Duarte, but backed out after the head of the Salvadoran Human Rights Commission, Herbert Anaya, was assassinated, believing that Duarte was not serious about curbing human rights abuses, meaningful economic reform or addressing the status of El Salvador as a vassalage to the United States. A coalition of religious organizations, led by the Catholic and Lutheran churches began to make a greater push for peace. Finally, Duarte's already questionable effectiveness as a leader diminished after he was diagnosed with terminal cancer.[3]

Murdered Jesuits, Crumbling Walls and the War's End

Another important election occurred in 1989. The leadership of ARENA realized that to have any chance at beating the Christian Democrats the party would need to continue to attempt to moderate its public image. Realizing that the Salvadoran public would never give what many perceived as the party of the death squads an electoral majority, the party bypassed Roberto D'Aubuisson as its candidate in favor of Alfredo Cristiani, himself a product of the oligarchy and educated in the United States, who had no political background in El Salvador and therefore no direct personal connections to the death squads. Skeptics charged that ARENA's efforts at moderation were a ruse and that D'Aubuisson was still in charge behind the scenes, citing as evidence D'Aubuisson's appearances at Cristiani's side during campaign events and his hand-picking the party's vice-presidential candidate. ARENA countered by trying to deflect attention from these issues by focusing on the corruption of the Duarte government and the hypocrisy of the Christian Democrats who had previously crusaded against such corruption before achieving power.

In early 1989, the FMLN advanced a proposal whereby the resistance would participate in the election, and accept its results, if the military were to stand down on election day, if absentee voting by exiles was permitted and if representatives of the Left were allowed onto El Salvador's Central Elections Council. After ARENA had negotiated with the resistance for several weeks, the latest round of peace talks broke down as ARENA was not able to agree on a timetable for holding the elections and backed out of further negotiations. The actual day of the election was rather violent, involving fighting between the army and the FMLN, a blackout in eighty percent of the country and a four-day transportation strike. Voter turnout decreased significantly from previous elections, and ARENA secured the presidency.[4]

Both ARENA and the FMLN began to moderate many of their positions as the 1990s began. Both sides realized that the Salvadoran people were tired of years of warfare and that to be perceived as an obstacle to the achievement of peace was to destroy whatever popular support either side possessed. President Cristiani called for a new round of talks with the rebels. Three separate meetings between Cristiani's representatives and the FMLN took place in late 1989, but a series of bombings of church and trade union offices convinced the resistance leadership that the Cristiani regime was insincere in its efforts at peace or, at best, had been unable to bring the military and the right-wing death squads under control. A number of dramatic events followed that eventually helped to pave the way to peace. The FMLN launched a major offensive in November of 1989. This proved to be one of the resistance's most effective actions in the entire history of the war, and discredited the claims of both U.S. and Salvadoran intelligence that the FMLN was finished as a capable fighting force. Instead, the rebels brought the war into the heart of the capital city of San Salvador, even occupying certain upper-class neighborhoods in the process. The army's efforts at retaliation proved too inept and impotent.

Four nights into the FMLN offensive, six Jesuit priests were killed, along with their housekeeper and her daughter, at the

Central America University. The perpetrators were members of the Atlacatl battalion, trained by the Americans and considered an elite military unit. This massacre generated the same international outrage as the massacre of the four churchwomen during the Carter era nine years earlier. The massacre demonstrated to many in the U.S. Congress that the El Salvador policy of the administration of Ronald Reagan and his successor, George H. W. Bush, had shown no fruit in nearly a decade. The massacre also produced a new round of international condemnation of U.S. policy in El Salvador. Once again, El Salvador figured prominently in the American media, and the atrocities produced outrage among sectors of the American public. Additionally, changes in the world at the time undermined the credibility of the claims of the American policy makers concerning Central America. Soviet Premier Mikhail Gorbachev had presided over a number of significant reforms in the Soviet Union and secured an important arms control agreement with President Reagan in the process. The FMLN offensive and the subsequent massacre of the Jesuits occurred during the same month that the "Velvet Revolution" began in Czechoslovakia, thereby setting in motion the chain of events that led to the eventual collapse of the Warsaw Pact and the tearing down of the Berlin Wall. Further, the largely pro-American opposition won an electoral victory over the Reagan administration's hated Sandinistas in the 1990 Nicaraguan election. [5] Given all that was transpiring in the world at the time, claims by the U.S. administration to be fighting for "democracy" and resisting Soviet expansionism in Central America took on an appearance of absurdity, even to many untrained or uninformed observers.

President Bush actually requested an increase in military aid from Congress in 1990, in order to counter the November 1989 offensive, but Congress proved to be resistant. Americas Watch issued a report at this time that offered the following summation of Reagan-Bush policies in El Salvador:

After nine years of stubborn defense of the Salvadoran

regime, and after more than $4 billion have been spent in propping it up, the urban offensive of November 1989 has put the Bush administration once again in the awkward position of defending the indefensible. It is clearly not enough to say that A. Cristiani is an elected official. If he has effective control over his country's armed and security forces, then he is ultimately responsible for the unspeakable abuses that those forces commit, as well as those committed by shadowy death squads with close links to his own political power. If he is in fact powerless to exert any meaningful control over them, then the Bush administration fiction that the U.S. supports a legitimate government is really no more than a thin veil to cover up its support of a murderous military.[6]

On October 19, 1990, the U.S. Congress voted to reduce military aid to El Salvador by fifty percent, with the remaining fifty being conditional on cooperation in the investigation of the murder of the Jesuit priests and good faith participation in peace talks with the FMLN.

The Aftermath and El Salvador Today

In 1991, the newly elected Nicaraguan President Violeta Chamorro delivered a new proposal for peace talks put forth by the FMLN. The proposal was presented to the chief diplomats of the Central American nations and the nations of the European Community, and received their endorsements, along with the endorsements of the U.S. Secretary of State James Baker and the Soviet Foreign Ministry. Peace negotiations subsequently began in Mexico with United Nations officials serving as mediators. The initial round of negotiations produced partial and tentative agreements for such measures as reform of El Salvador's judiciary and electoral system, civilian control over the military and police, and efforts to seriously investigate matters of major human rights abuses. Sensing that the end of the war was near, some far right-wing Salvadoran groups escalated their terrorist and death squad activities, though the Salvadoran government came under tremendous pressure to end the war from both the United States and from a variety of Latin American nations. Former President Duarte had since passed away due to his cancer, and the right-wing leader D'Aubuisson was by now also terminally ill with throat cancer. The two leading Salvadoran political figures from the war period were now irrelevant. President Cristiani met in New York City with representatives of the State Department of U.S. President Bush on December 29, 1991 and U.S. officials expressed their desire for an end to the war. Further negotiations took place between representatives of the Salvadoran government and the FMLN at the United Nations. Finally, peace accords were signed by the two sides in Mexico City on January 16, 1992.[7]

A ceasefire had begun on December 31, 1991 and was never broken. The final provisions of the peace accords included the reduction of the Salvadoran armed forces by fifty percent, incorporation of the FMLN guerrillas into the police, recognition of the FMLN as a political party, land reform and the expulsion of the worst human rights violators from the military. Plans were also drawn for the "reconstruction" of Salvadoran society that had been devastated by the war and repression, primarily by rebuilding infrastructure, schools and medical facilities. Some provision was also made for partially separate government of FMLN-controlled regions and those that had remained directly under the Salvadoran state throughout the course of the war. A United Nations Truth Commission released its report in March of 1993 and the report included findings that Roberto D'Aubuisson had been responsible for the assassination of Archbishop Romero in 1980, the murder of the four churchwomen in 1980 had been planned, carried out and covered up by senior members of the National Guard, the U.S. trained Atlacatl battalion had been responsible for the El Mozote massacre in 1981, and high-ranking military officers had been responsible for the massacre of the Jesuits in 1989.[8]

Another major election was held in El Salvador in 1994, with this being the first in which the FMLN participated. The results of the election were disappointing to the political Left as ARENA was the winner of the popular vote, with the FMLN coming in a distant second, and the Christian Democrats in third place. The new President was Armando Calderon Sol, an admirer and former associate of Roberto D'Aubuisson. The victory of the political Right was a surprise to many. Numerous claims of electoral fraud emerged. The United Nations estimated that as much as twenty percent of the electorate, mostly from the lower classes, did not receive a voting card, thereby rendering them ineligible. Approximately 74,000 people were disqualified for lacking a birth certificate, in some cases because records offices had been destroyed in the fighting that had consumed El Salvador for over a decade. Polling places were frequently located in distant places, and bus companies owned by ARENA sympathizers hindered transportation services on election day. Many voters were disqualified for minor irregularities, like the misspelling of the names on voter registration rolls. Sometimes the polls would simply close before everyone waiting in line had a chance to vote. Soldiers loyal to ARENA also attempted to intimidate voters from poor areas.[9]

ARENA possessed both more money and more experience with political campaigns, and was therefore able to run a more efficient campaign, while appealing to fears of communism and pointing to the alleged economic inefficiency of the Sandinista government in Nicaragua. The FMLN was less belligerent in its rhetoric, pointing less to ARENA's past ties to the death squads and more on positive reform efforts. The FMLN also failed to run in coalition with other left-wing groups, thereby producing a split in the left-wing vote, particularly in municipal elections. ARENA continues to dominate the politics of El Salvador in 2009, having won the most recent presidential election in 2004. The FMLN continues to be a competitive opposition party, though it has been weakened by internal splits and ideological disputes. While the FMLN has yet to win the presidency, it has at times controlled the legislative assembly, and the current mayor of the capital city of San Salvador, Violeta Menjivar, is an FMLN member and the first woman to hold the mayoral position.

While many of the sharp class divisions between the oligarchy, army and business community and the poor, working class and peasantry remain, significant developments have occurred in El Salvador since the chaotic years of the 1970s and the subsequent civil war that lasted for over a decade. Political freedom has increased significantly, and the political Left is allowed a seat at the political table. Popular organizations can operate with reduced fear of harsh repression. The status of women has improved somewhat and the religious communities in El Salvador are able to play a progressive social role, and the oligarchy has had to make certain concessions in order to guarantee its future survival in the face of potential revolution.[10]

1   Duarte, pp. 177-208.

2   Lydia Chavez, "Salvador to Restructure Security Forces," *New York Times*, June 14, 1984; Robert J. McCartney, "Duarte Tries Again in El Salvador," *Washington Post*, March 15, 1984; Nairn, pp. 20ff; Montgomery, pp. 183-191.

3   Nancy Cooper and Joseph Contreras, "A Major Win for Duarte," *Newsweek*, April 15, 1985; Robert J. McCartney, "U.S. Cools Support for Duarte," *Washington Post*, March 20, 1985; Montgomery, pp.192-211; Chris Norton, "Duarte Election Win Thwarts Right Wing," *In These Times*, April 17-23, 1985.

4   Montgomery, pp. 213, 215.

5   Noam Chomsky, *Deterring Democracy* (New York: Hill and Wang, 1992), pp. 298-300.

6   *Americas Watch*, cited in Montgomery, pp. 215- 220.

7   Montgomery, pp. 224-225.

8   Montgomery, p. 242-243

9   Blum, pp. 368-69.

10   Montgomery, p. 256.

Assessment and Conclusion

General Assessment

This book has attempted to address five principal questions concerning the Salvadoran civil war of the 1980s and its relationship to U.S. foreign policy. It has been shown that the roots of the Salvadoran civil war can be found in previously existing relationships of both political and economic oppression within domestic Salvadoran society itself and a hegemonic international relationship between El Salvador and the imperial power of the United States. These combined forces of domestic oppression and international subjugation essentially created a "powder keg" effect that eventually erupted into civil war in 1980. The civil war was not inevitable, and it might have been avoided had either the Salvadoran oligarchy or the American policy makers, or both, made some honest and comprehensive efforts to address the issues in Salvadoran society which led to such a high level of acrimony, volatility and violence. Many occasions for genuine reform presented themselves in the decades leading up to the civil war. For instance, if the Salvadoran elite had responded to the uprising of 1932 by granting significant concessions and implementing substantive reforms, the situation would not have deteriorated so radically in the decades ahead. Likewise, if efforts by genuinely reform minded governments, such as those that came to power in the coups of 1960 and 1979 or the opposition coalition that was cheated out of its electoral victory in 1972, had been allowed to maintain power, then the social pressures that ultimately led to war might have been at least partially defused.[1]

The American client-state system in Latin America bears considerable but only partial blame for both the social, political and economic conditions that led to the wars in Central America in the 1980s. Clearly, the local oligarchies were tyrannical and exploitative enough in their own right and this problem would have persisted even if American influence had largely been absent and, indeed, it has been shown that American policy towards its Latin American client-states and prospective client-states has vacillated between aggression and attempts at consolidated hegemony on one end and neglect on the other. Yet, it has also been shown that American hegemony and the client-state system that is its foundation has perpetually served to not only reinforce the oppressive tendencies of local oligarchies, but to reinforce those tendencies by strengthening such oligarchies and by imposing substantial obstacles to political, economic and social development or progress. American imperial hegemony is yet another layer of oppression inflicted upon Latin American societies *on top of and in addition to* oppression maintained by local regimes and the ruling classes whom they represent.

With regards to the Salvadoran civil war itself, the performance of the Carter administration illustrates how American hegemony has strengthened regional oppression, exacerbated already existing class and political conflicts and contributed to an atmosphere of political chaos, violence and social deterioration beyond even what would have already been generated by regional and local conditions in Central America generally and El Salvador specifically. There can be no denying that the increased concern for human rights *initially* demonstrated by the Carter administration produced tangible successes in certain areas as even honest conservatives in the U.S. (such as William F. Buckley, Jr.) admitted. However, it has also been shown that the Carter administration's concern for human rights was always subordinated to the preservation of American imperial hegemony generally and the client-state system specifically, not only in Central America but in other regions, even to the point of absurd betrayal of Carter's human rights stance and America's supposed anti-communist ideological superstructure for the sake of lending support to barbarians such as the Khmer Rouge. This subordination of human rights issues to broader geopolitical concerns escalated sharply as the Carter administration progressed. The key failure of the Carter administration in El Salvador, beyond the inconsistency and weakness in its human rights policy, was its failure to support the reformist coup of October, 1979. If the Carter administration had simply demanded that the reform-minded elements within the coup be allowed to pursue their program of reform, and made continued American aid contingent upon such, then the political situation in El Salvador would likely have not fallen into such complete disarray. Yet the principal aim of the Carter administration was not the prevention of civil war or the upholding of human rights, but maintenance of the client-state system and broader American hegemony, and avoiding a repeat of the Nicaraguan revolution of July, 1979. Indeed, the failure of President Carter and his administration to heed the pleas of Archbishop Romero serves as one of the greatest and most shameful failures of the Carter administration and is a major blight on Carter's legacy.

While it is clear enough that the Salvadoran civil war not only begun but escalated during the Carter era, and that the policies of the Carter administration contributed mightily to the escalation, a clear line of distinction should be drawn between the administrations of Carter and Ronald Reagan. In some ways, the policies of the Reagan administration concerning El Salvador were not only a continuation but *intensification* of policies begun by the Carter administration. Both administrations had the preservation of American hegemony and the client-state system and the prevention of anti-imperialist revolutions as their primary foreign policy objective in Central America (and virtually everywhere else). Both administrations subordinated human rights issues to geopolitical considerations. Both administrations continued to aid the Salvadoran regime even though the bloodthirsty nature of that regime was apparent enough. Yet it has been shown that the Reagan administration was also a *departure* from the Carter administration in a number of ways. Perhaps the greatest illustration of this is the firing of Ambassador Robert White by Secretary of State Alexander Haig. Ambassador White, whatever the deficiencies of his perception of the political situation and armed conflict in El

Salvador, clearly demonstrated genuine concern for the human rights issues in that country, particularly after the murder of the four churchwomen in 1980. Ambassador White became a critic of the Salvadoran ruling class' horrific human rights policies, and did so at considerable professional as well as physical risk. There were no figures comparable to Ambassador White to be found in the circle of Reagan administration policy makers for El Salvador. Instead, it has been shown that those appointed to key positions concerning U.S. policy in El Salvador by the Reagan administration were notably lacking in the appropriate levels of experience, expertise, or skill, with some of them being astoundingly incompetent.

The disregard for human rights and the atrocities perpetrated by the Salvadoran state, army and oligarchy were widely known and widely documented even in the earliest phases of the war and, indeed, such atrocities were certainly not original to the civil war period but had taken place for decades prior to that. It has been shown that the Reagan administration knew of the extent of such atrocities, not only from the reports of human rights organizations and the media at large, but from its own internal intelligence and information provided directly from the American embassy in El Salvador. The Reagan administration first sought to deny the existence of these atrocities, and then sought to minimize their importance, prevalence or significance. When such denial was no longer feasible, the Reagan administration feigned at least partial fidelity to human rights principles, and claimed due diligence in reducing such atrocities in El Salvador, all the while seeking to undermine efforts by the U.S. Congress and others to curb the occurrence of further atrocities. Indeed, it has been shown that the Reagan administration had no interest whatsoever in human rights issues pertaining to El Salvador, seeking at first to obscure the issue and then recognizing the issue only on the most superficial level as a means of saving political face and protecting its own policy objectives. As Kathryn Sikkink observes:

Basically, Reagan had been so rhetorically supportive of the worldview of the right in Central America that right-wing leaders didn't believe that the Reagan administration would cut aid. By rhetorically embracing the right without asking for any concessions in return, in other words, the Reagan administration, gave away bargaining leverage it might have used. When the embassies in Guatemala City or San Salvador began expressing concern over human rights, the military and the right in these countries thought that the problem was with the embassies. They never doubted they had the support of Reagan.[2]

The evidence is overwhelming that "the military and the right in these countries" were correct in their assessment of the intentions of the Reagan administration's policy makers.

The Free World Versus Communism or American Imperialism Verses Third World Nationalism?

This work's examination of the origin and nature of the Salvadoran resistance provides additional insights and raises additional questions into not only the nature and function of American foreign policy in Central America during the time period examined, but also into the broader role of American hegemony in the Southern Hemisphere generally and in other regions of the world, such as the Middle East, Africa or Asia. It has been shown that regard for human rights considerations was present though inconsistent during the Carter period, and deteriorated considerably with time, only to be eradicated almost completely with the advent of the Reagan administration. However, a much wider question concerns the matter of whether or not the advancement of human rights is compatible with the maintenance of American hegemony on any serious or permanent level? Or does the failure, inconsistency and, finally, abandonment of human rights considerations altogether demonstrated by the Carter and Reagan administrations reflect an inevitable consequence of the maintenance of the hegemonic order of the client-state system?

The evidence that has been accumulated in this study indicates that the primary efforts to advance human rights, social progress and economic and political "justice" in El Salvador were those of the Salvadoran resistance. Whatever contributions the makers of American foreign policy may have made in this area are clearly overshadowed by the obstacles to such advances created by American policy. It has been shown that the Salvadoran resistance was an improvement on many previous Third World "national liberation" struggles against Western imperialism. The Salvadoran rebels exhibited none of the passion for ruthless or predatory violence of groups such as Peru's Shining Path or Cambodia's Khmer Rouge.[3] Nor did the Salvadoran resistance demonstrate the Stalinist loyalties of the Cubans or Vietnamese, or the reactionary Islamic outlook of many resistance movements in the Middle East.[4] Indeed, the Salvadoran resistance only took up arms against the state when all other options had been fully exhausted and only when opposition forces were faced with total extermination. Even at that, the resistance made repeated efforts to negotiate for peace on the condition of reasonable reforms, only to be rejected by the Salvadoran elite and, perhaps just as vehemently, by the Americans.

The evidence is also clear that it was the U.S. foreign policy makers that were the principal obstacle to the achievement of peace in El Salvador. The continued funding of the Salvadoran war effort against the resistance enhanced the ability of the Salvadoran state and armed forces to maintain their position when they would likely have either fallen or fought to a stalemate without American aid. If U.S. assistance had simply been cut off as it became clear that efforts towards reform and purging the Salvadoran government and army of its most criminal elements would not be forthcoming, then the Salvadoran regime would have had no choice but to make substantial concessions as part of a peace settlement or face its probable overthrow. It is also clear enough that American policy in El Salvador was driven by considerations other than those rooted in Cold War geopolitics. Efforts by the United States to dominate Central America extend back much further than the beginning of the Cold War, or even the Bolshevik Revolution of 1917. Cold War rhetoric simply provided a smokescreen for pursuing a hegemonic policy extending back to the nineteenth century. Indeed, members of the U.S. foreign policy establishment with the requisite level of professional experience and personal candor would frequently point out that the United States had no legitimate or essential interests in El Salvador of the kind that would warrant the policies pursued by the Carter administration in the early period of the civil war or the Reagan and Bush administrations for more than a decade after the war began.

The insincerity of the U.S. foreign policy makers' Cold War rationale was demonstrated in a good number of ways, but there are several that stand out as pertinent examples. Among these are fraudulent claims and forgeries found in the "white paper" issued in 1981 by the Reagan administration, the findings of intelligence professionals that contradicted the claims of the policy makers, and the contents of documents captured directly from the Salvadoran resistance that indicated Nicaraguan involvement in the Salvadoran revolution was minimal, Cuban involvement even less, and Soviet involvement near non-existent. A poignant piece of evidence of the policy makers' insincerity is the fact that the George H. W. Bush administration actually asked for an *increase* in aid to El Salvador *in 1990 after* the Cold War had virtually ended. The pro-Soviet states of Eastern Europe had fallen apart without Soviet intervention, and President Reagan and Soviet Premiere Mikhail Gorbachev had publicly embraced after securing an arms control treaty.[5]

The Cold War rationale also involved a number of other dubious presumptions. One of these was Jeane Kirkpatrick's "dictatorships and double standards" thesis, which claimed that "communist" regimes were not amenable to reform, while right-wing dictatorships of the kind favored by the U.S. were, therefore the latter deserved support as a bulwark against the former. This thesis was roundly debunked by the events in the Soviet Union and Eastern Europe in the late 1980s, by the reforms implemented in China following the demise of Maoism,[6] and subsequent reforms in Vetnam. Kirkpatrick's hypocrisy and dubious sincerity concerning such claims were also made evident by her steadfast defense of recognition of the Pol Pot regime as the legitimate government of Cambodia. [7]

Former U.S. Secretary of State George Shultz was widely regarded as one of the more moderate members of the Reagan administration, having replaced Alexander Haig, whose reputation was that of a right-wing ideologue. In his memoirs, Shultz described what he regarded as having been the Reagan administration's primary dilemmas in El Salvador:

A major problem in our assistance to El Salvador was "certification," which could stop us dead in our tracks at any time. "Certification" was Congress's way of saying it would curtail the funds needed in Central America unless we could demonstrate that notorious problems in the countries we supported were being solved, particularly the implementation of land reform in El Salvador, the elimination of "death squads," and progress in bringing to justice those in El Salvador who had murdered American nuns and representatives of the AFL-CIO. What this amounted to was congressional micromanagement of the U.S. economic and security assistance program. Funds were appropriated which would be released for a period of six months. Before the next six-month increment could be released, the secretary of state had to certify that progress was being made on the human rights and rule-of-law aspects of life in El Salvador. We were constantly struggling with an excruciating dilemma: on the one hand, we could point to progress; on the other hand, there were still great and disturbing problems. So we would certify the progress, but we realized that many thorny and deeply troublesome difficulties remained.

At the same time, from the standpoint of the Salvadoran military, certification created a problem. The military had funds and resources available to them for six months; they did not know if these resources would be renewed for another six months. Because of this uncertainty, quite predictably they husbanded their resources and therefore did not use them as effectively as possible to contend with the guerrillas. And as a result, Congress said that the security assistance was wasted because it was not being effectively used. It was a vicious circle. We argued for a longer time horizon so that the Salvadoran military could plan ahead and make better use of their resources. But Congress was reluctant. The governments of El Salvador, Honduras, Guatemala contained and tolerated many unsavory characters. Still, serious people in those governments were engaged in a stalwart effort to move toward democracy and the rule of law. The American left would have us leave those governments to struggle on their own and not worry whether communism came to prevail. The American right would have us support the anti-Communists no matter how outrageous their behavior. [8]

It has been established that the American regime in whom Shultz was the top ranking diplomat did indeed "support the anti-Communists no matter how outrageous their behavior." It is clear that for Shultz the primary considerations were maintaining American hegemony in El Salvador and other Central American nations by defeating "the Communists" and preserving the Salvadoran armed forces as effective fighters. Clearly, Shultz regarded Congressional concerns for human rights in the region, tepid even though these may have at times been, as more of a nuisance and irritation than a matter of pressing concern. It has also been shown in this study that Shultz's claim that "serious people in those governments were engaged in a stalwart effort to move toward democracy and the rule of law" is a rather dubious one. Such figures were actually very rare in the Salvadoran political establishment and when they did emerge, the reform minded officers of the 1979 coup being an example, the U.S. either ignored or sought to undermine them.

Further, Shultz's reference to "democracy and the rule of law" involves a use of these terms that is highly subjective at best and more likely exceedingly hollow. It was revealed in the official documents as well as captured private documents of the Salvadoran resistance that the economic program of the FMLN-FDR was essentially a combination of agrarian reform, peasant populism, progressive Catholicism and European-style social democracy, and far removed from the command economies associated with orthodox Marxism-Leninism. The rebels in fact attempted to initiate negotiations for a peace agreement on numerous occasions, with provision for open public elections. On those occasions during the civil war and its aftermath that elections were officially held, it was the forces of the Salvadoran right-wing and its supporters that sought to undermine the electoral process, and exclude genuine opposition parties and popular organizations from participating. Indeed, the Christian "base communities" and the proposals of the resistance for a system of local self-rule and democratic participation provided a foundation for a form of democratic politics that, if fully implemented, would be more progressive than the parliamentary or representative systems found in the "advanced" countries.[9] As for "rule of law," it has been shown that the rebel forces in fact created a functional alternative infrastructure of their own, including a legal infrastructure, which was vastly superior to the bloodthirsty lawlessness of the Salvadoran state itself.

Relevance of the Salvadoran Civil War to Contemporary U.S. Foreign Policy and International Relations

For a historian of international relations or American foreign policy, one of the most interesting aspects of the relationship between the Salvadoran civil war and the foreign policy of the United States during the same period is the way in which this relationship provides a classic case study in modern imperialism. No clearer an example of a Third World nation struggling for self-determination and political, economic and social development against an oppressive local oligarchy and its international benefactors and overlords is available. Greg Gandin describes the ideological legacy of U.S. policy towards Latin America during the Cold War:

> Latin America…plays a curious role in current geopolitical debates taking place in the United States. The Right sees the region as a success story: following the 1959 Cuban Revolution, the United States, facing an insurgent blend of Marxism and militant nationalism, responded with an effective mix of hard and soft power, neutralized the opposition, and transformed most of the continent's nations into free market allies and their populations into willing consumers of U.S. goods and technology…

The Left of course draws a different lesson. For those who unequivocally oppose military interventions abroad, the sad history of U.S. hemispheric policy is a self-evident confirmation of their position. Others, however, who support some version of the "war on terror" in the name of progressive values, while admitting the base motives and baleful legacy of the United States in the region, argue that the past does not necessarily have to determine the future. And besides, according to this perspective, even if Washington is driven by less than noble purpose, it does not follow that its power could not achieve some good-to stem religious intolerance, for example, or to stop massive human rights abuses and overthrow indefensible dictatorships in an increasingly volatile and dangerous world.[10]

This debate is particularly pertinent given that the foundations of contemporary American foreign policy are in many ways a continuation of previous policies in such places as Central America. Even some of the same individuals associated with Reagan administration policy in Central America, such as Elliot Abrams and John Negroponte, reemerged within the neoconservative circle surrounding President George W. Bush.[11]

The man who was arguably most responsible for the hawkish turn of the Carter administration, Zbigniew Brzezinski, has thus far been at least an informal advisor to President Barack Obama.[12] With the end of the Cold War, American militarism has escalated without the restraining presence of the Soviet Union. Much of the same Cold War rhetoric used to legitimize American policy in places like El Salvador has been recycled under the cover of the "war on terror" and shifted its focus towards the Middle East. "Democracy" and "human rights" are invoked, along with anti-terrorism appeals, as justifications for American military action against insurgent movements worldwide, and even as rationales for American imperial hegemony.[13] Consequently, a truthful and factual understanding concerning what really transpired regarding U.S. foreign policy in El Salvador and other Central American nations during the 1980s, and the wider context of the effect of American power in Latin America generally, is essential to an informed and substantive evaluation of the claims of current U.S. policy makers, and the likely effects of their policies. As Grandin summarizes:

> In Latin America, in country after country, the mass peasant and working class movements that gained ground in the middle of the twentieth century were absolutely indispensable to the advancement of democracy. To the degree that Latin America today may be considered democratic, it was the Left, including the Marxist Left, that made it so. Empire, rather than fortifying democracy, weakened it. Launched first by domestic elites in the years after World War II and then quickly joined by the United States, the savage crusade, justified under the guise of the Cold War, against Latin American democratic movements had devastating human and political costs. In some countries, such as Uruguay, Brazil and Chile, national

security states carried out focuses, surgically precise repression. Other states, such as Argentina, El Salvador, and Guatemala, let loose a more scattershot horror.[14]

Likewise, genuine political, economic and social development and advancement in places such as Iraq, Afghanistan, Africa, South Asia or elsewhere will likely be the results of indigenous struggles rooted in the social circumstances and cultural particularities of those nations or regions, with American power serving as a hindering force rather than playing a facilitative role, and with such advancements being in part dependent on the retreat rather than extension of American power. [15]

1   Blum, pp. 353-357.

2   Kathryn Sikkink, *Mixed Signals: U.S. Human Rights Policy and Latin America* (Ithaca: Cornell University Press, 2004), p. 170.

3   Jeremy McDermott, "Return of Peru's Shining Path as Terror Movement Kills 19 Soldiers," *The Daily Telegraph*, London, October 11, 2008; Philip Short, Pol Pot: Anatomy of a Nightmare (Henry Colt and Company, 2005).

4   Mitchell Prothero, "Hezbollah Strengthens Its Grip in Lebanon," *U. S. News & World Report*, August 4, 2008.

5   David K. Shipler, "Reagan and Gorbachev Sign Missile Treaty and Vow to Work for Greater Reductions," *New York Times*, December 9, 1987.

6   Justin Raimondo, "China and the New Cold War," *Antiwar.Com*, June 17, 1999. Archived at http://www.antiwar.com/justin/justinchina1.html Accessed on January 8, 2008.

7   Peter H. McGuire, *Facing Death in Cambodia* (New York: Columbia University Press, 2005), pp. 72-75.

8   George P. Shultz, *Turmoil and Triumph: My Years as Secretary of State* (New York: Charles Scribner's Sons, 1993), pp. 290-291.

9   Hans Hermann Hoppe, *Democracy: The God That Failed* (London: Transaction Publishers, 2001).

10   Greg Gandin, *The Last Colonial Massacre: Latin America in the Cold War* (Chicago and London: University of Chicago, 2004), pp. xiii-xiv.

11   Michael Lind, "The Weird Men Behind Bush's War," *New Statesman*, London, April 4, 2003.

12   Webster Tarpley, "Confirmed-Obama is Zbigniew Brzezinski Puppet,"

Assessment and Conclusion

Commentary, March 21, 2008.

13   Noam Chomsky, *The New Military Humanism: Lessons From Kosovo* (Common Courage Press, 2002).

14   Grandin, pp. xiv-xv.

15   Blum, pp. 383-393.

Letter from Archbishop Romero to President Carter

February 17th, 2005 marked the 25th anniversary of Archbishop Oscar Romero's letter to President Jimmy Carter asking him not to send military aid to El Salvador. Five weeks later Romero was assassinated. Two days following Romero's funeral, the U.S. House Appropriations Subcommittee on Foreign Operations approved Carter's request for "non lethal" military aid to El Salvador. This letter still resonates today as the "Salvador Option" is considered as a strategy in Iraq.

Mr. President:

In these last days there has appeared in the national press a report that troubles me deeply. According to it, your government is studying the possibility of supporting and aiding economically and militarily the government junta [of El Salvador].

Because you are a Christian and because you manifested that you wish to defend human rights, I dare to expose my pastoral point of view regarding this news and make a concrete petition to you.

I am deeply troubled by the news that the government of the United States should be studying the way to favor the militarist path of El Salvador by sending military equipment and advisors to "train three Salvadoran battallions in logistics, communications and intelligence." In the event that this journalistic information is true, your government's contribution, rather than favoring greater justice and peace in El Salvador will make injustice and repression against the organization of the people, who have been struggling for the respect of their most fundamental rights, even more accute.

The current ruling Junta, and above all the armed forces and security forces, have unfortunately not demonstrated their capacity to resolve the grave national problems through political practice and structural means. In general, they have only resorted to repressive violence, producing a volume of dead and wounded that is greater than that of recent military regimes whose systematic violation of human rights was condemned by the Interamerican Commission on Human Rights.

The brutal way in which the security forces recently evicted and assassinated the occupants of the headquarters of the Christian Democratic Party despite that the Junta and the government (it would appear) did not authorize that operation is evidence that the Junta and the Christian Democrats do not govern the country, but rather, the political power is in the hands of military men without scruples, who only know how to oppress the people and favor the interests of the Salvadoran oligarchy.

If it is true that this past November, "a group of six Americans spent time in El Salvador supplying two hundred thousand dollars worth of gas masks and bullet proof vests and instructing on their use against demonstrators, you yourself must know that clearly since then the security forces, acting with greater personal protection and effectiveness, have repressed the people even more violently, using deadly weapons.

As such, given the fact that as a Salvadoran, and as Archbishop of the Archdiocese of San Salvador, I have the obligation to watch so that faith and justice reign in my country, I ask that if you truly want to defend human rights:

• You prohibit this military aid to the Salvadoran government.
• You guarantee that your government not intervene directly or indirectly with military, economic and diplomatic pressure.

At this time, we are living through a grave economic and political crisis in our country, but it is doubtless that each time the people have increased their conscience and their organization and have empowered themselves to become the driving force which is responsible for the future of El Salvador, and the only one capable of overcoming this crisis.

It would be unjust and deplorable that by the interference of foreign powers the Salvadoran people were frustrated, they were repressed, and impeded in deciding with autonomy over the economic and political trajectory that our country should follow. It would supose violating a right that the Latin American bishops gathered in Puebla publicly acknowledged when we said: "The legitimate self-determination of our countries that permits them to organize according to their own disposition and history, and to cooperate in a new international order..." (Puebla Synod, 505.)

I hope that your religious convictions and your sensibilities in defense of human rights will compel you to accept my petition, avoiding with it a major spilling of blood in my long-suffered country.

Yours truly,

Oscar A. Romero (Archbishop)

Bibliography

Primary Sources

Amnesty International, *Torture in the Eighties*

Covert Action Information Bulletin, Archives

Human Rights Commission on El Salvador (CDHES)

Human Rights Report, Archives on El Salvador

Report of The Commission on the Truth for El Salvador

Government Documents

CIA World Fact Book. Accessed March 22, 2008. Archived at https://www.cia.gov/library/publications/the-world-factbook/index.html

"Dissent Paper on El Salvador and Central America", reprinted in Warner Poelchau, ed., *White Paper, Whitewash* (New York, 1981).

Epstein, Susan B., Nina M. Serafina and Frances T. Miko. *Democracy Promotion: Cornerstone of U.S. Foreign Policy?* Prepared for Members of Congress. Congressional Research Service: December 26, 2007.

House Subcommittee on Oversight and Evaluation, Permanent Select Committee on Intelligence, *U.S. Intelligence Performance on Central America:Achievements and Selected Instances of Concern*, Staff Report, September, 22, 1982.

Immigration and Naturalization Service Resource Information, Master Exhibit Series, *El Salvador: Persecution by Death Squads and Security Services/Special Forces*, October, 1997.

National Security Archives, *El Salvador: War, Peace, and Human Rights, 1980-1994* (declassified).

National Security Archives, *El Salvador: The Making of U.S. Policy,1977-1984*, microfiche collection.

National Security Archive, "Interview with President Jimmy Carter", *Backyard: Episode 18*, Archived at http://www.gwu.edu/~nsarchiv/coldwar/interviews/episode-18/carter3.html.

North American Congress on Latin America, *NACLA Report on the Americas.*

Report of the President's National Bipartisan Commission on Central America.

United Nations Department of Public Information, *The United Nations and El Salvador 1990-1995.*

El Salvador - A War by Proxy

United States State Department, *Communist Interference in El Salvador*, White Paper, February 23, 1981.

United States State Department and Department of Defense, *Background Paper: Nicaragua's Military Build-Up and Support for Central American Subversion*, July 18, 1984.

United States State Department, *Revolution Beyond Our Borders*, September, 1985.

Newspapers and Magazines

Commentary

Commonweal

El Dia (Mexico)

El Diario de Hoy (San Salvador)

Extra! - Newsletter of FAIR (Fairness and Accuracy in Reporting)

Foreign Policy

Human Rights Quarterly

LA Weekly

Los Angeles Times

National Catholic Reporter

Newsweek

New York Times

Overthrow

Playboy (November 1984)

Political Science Quarterly

San Francisco Chronicle

San Francisco Examiner

Stanford Daily

Tanbou

Time

The Atlantic

The Guardian (London)

The Iranian

The Nation

The Progressive

Bibliography

The New Yorker

The Spectator (London)

Third World Quarterly

US News and World Report

Wall Street Journal

Washington Post

Z Magazine

Secondary Sources

Articles

Arnson, Cynthia, "Background Information on El Salvador and U.S. Military Assistance to Central America," Update no. 4, Institute for Policy Studies, Washington, D.C., April 1981 (memo).

Behrooz, Maziar "Surprise: Nobody Saw the Revolution Coming", *The Iranian*, February 22, 2001.

Brodhead, Frank, "Demonstration Elections in El Salvador," in Marvin E. Gettleman, et. al., *El Salvador: Central America in the New Cold War*, rev. ed. New York: Grove Press, 1986.

Chavez, Lydia, "Salvador to Restructure Security Forces," *New York Times,* June 14, 1984.

Chitnis, Lord, "Observing El Salvador: The 1984 Elections", *Third World Quarterly*, October 1984.

Cohen, Jeff and Norman Solomon, "Jimmy Carter and Human Rights: Behind the Media Myth", *Media Beat*, (Fairness and Accuracy in Reporting), September 21, 1994.

Cooper, Nancy and Joseph Contreras, "A Major Win for Duarte," *Newsweek,* April 15, 1985

DeRienzo, Paul, "A Salvadoran Refugee Speaks", *Overthrow*, May, 1984.

Dinges, John, "Salvadoran Rebels Hold Base," *Washington Post,* January 22, 1982.

Dinges, John, "White Paper or Blank Paper?" *Los Angeles Times*, March 17.

Drehsler, Alex, "Guerrillas Use Guns to Forge Marxist Society," *San Diego Union,* March 2, 1981.

Drehsler, Alex, "Revolution or Death!" *San Diego Union*, March 1, 1981.

Eldon, Eric, "International Spotlight: El Salvador", *Stanford Daily*, March 3, 2003.

Elias, Robert, "Terrorism and American Foreign Policy", *Tanbou*, September 25, 2001.

Engler, Mark, "Crimes in Freedom's Name: Dick Cheney's El Salvador", *Z Magazine*, October 8, 2004.

Fisher, Stewart W, "Human Rights in El Salvador and U. S. Foreign Policy", *Human Rights Quarterly*, Vol. 4, No. 1 (Spring, 1982), pp. 1-38.

Forche, Carolyn, "The Road to Reaction in El Salvador", *The Nation* (New York), June 14, 1980.

Gibb, Tom, "El Salvador Verdicts Could Open Floodgates", *BBC News*, July 24, 2002.

Gibb, Tom, "Salvadoreans Remember Slain Cleric", *BBC News*, March 25, 2000.

Gibb, Tom, "U.S. Role in Salvador's Brutal War", *BBC News*, March 24, 2002.

Gutierrez, Raul, "Amnesty Law Biggest Obstacle to Human Rights, Activists Say", *Inter Press Service News Agency*, May 19, 2007.

Huntington, Samuel, "American Ideals Versus American Institutions", *Political Science Quarterly*, Spring, 1982.

Jones, Arthur, "El Salvador Revisited: a Look at Declassified State Department Documents - Some of What U.S. Government Knew - and When It Knew It",

National Catholic Reporter, September 23, 1994.

Kahn, Jeffrey, "Ronald Reagan launched his political career using the Berkeley campus as a target", *UCBerkeley News*, June 8, 2004.

Kaiser, Robert G. "White Paper on El Salvador is Faulty," *Washington Post*, June 9, 1981.

Kirkpatrick, Jeane J., "Dictatorships and Double Standards", *Commentary*, November, 1979.

Krause, Cliffard, "How U.S. Actions Helped Hide Salvador Human Rights Abuses", *New York Times*, March 21, 1993.

Kwitney, Jonathan, "Apparent Errors Cloud U.S. 'White Paper' on Reds in El Salvador, *Wall Street Journal*, June 8, 1981.

Lind, Michael, "The Weird Men Behind Bush's War," *New Statesman*, London, April 4, 2003.

McCartney, Robert J. "Duarte Tries Again in El Salvador," *Washington Post*, March 15, 1984.

McCartney, Robert J. "U.S. Cools Support for Duarte," *Washington Post*, March 20, 1985.

Bibliography

McDermott, Jeremy. "Return of Peru's Shining Path as Terror Movement Kills 19 Soldiers," *Telegraph*, London, October 11, 2008.

McGehee, Ralph, "The CIA and the White Paper on El Salvador," *The Nation*, April 11, 1981.

Miller, George, "El Salvador: Policy of Deceit", *New York Times*, October 21, 1988.

Muravchik, Joshua, "Marx Meet Oedipus," *National Review*, May 8, 2002.

Nairn, Allan, "Behind the Death Squads", *The Progressive*, May 1984.

Norton, Chris, "Duarte Election Win Thwarts Right Wing," *In These Times*, April 17-23, 1985.

O'Brien-Steinfels, Margaret, "Death and Lies in El Salvador: The Ambassador's Tale-Robert White-Interview", *Commonweal*, October 26, 2001.

Petras, James, "White Paper on the White Paper," *The Nation*, March 28, 1981.

Pilger, John, "How Thatcher Gave Pol Pot a Hand", *New Statesman*, April 17, 2000. Archived at http://www.newstatesman.com/200004170017, Accessed on October 5, 2008.

Prothero, Mitchell. "Hezbollah Strengthens Its Grip in Lebanon," *U. S. News & World Report*, August 4, 2008.

Pyes, Craig, "The New American Right Picks Up a Hot Potato," *Albuquerque Journal*, December 22, 1983.

Raimondo, Justin."China and the New Cold War," *Antiwar.Com*, June 17, 1999. Archived at http://www.antiwar.com/justin/justinchina1.html Accessed on January 8, 2008.

Reese, Charley. "A Giant is Dead", *Ottawa Herald*, August 11, 2008.

Rich, Don A.,"The American Empire is Another Bubble", Ludwig von Mises Institute, September 12, 2008. Archived at http://mises.org/story/3095. Schwarz, Benjamin. "Dirty Hands", *The Atlantic*, December, 1998.

David K. Shipler. "Reagan and Gorbachev Sign Missile Treaty and Vow to Work for Greater Reductions," *New York Times*, December 9, 1987.

Shultz, George P., "Secretary's Interview on "Meet the Press", *US Department of State Bulletin*, May, 1984.

Tarpley, Webster. "Confirmed-Obama is Zbigniew Brzezinski Puppet," *Commentary*, March 21, 2008.

Taylor, Robert W. and Harry E. Vanden, "Defining Terrorism in El Salvador: 'La Mantanza'", *The ANNALS of the American Academy of Political and Social Science* Vol. 463, No. 1, 106-118, 1982.

Thornton, Mark,"Skyscrapers and Business Cycles", *Journal of Austrian Economics*, vol. 8, no. 1, Spring, 2005.

Wilson, Michael G.,"Reagan and Bush Policies Are Paying Off in El Salvador", *Backgrounder #983*, Heritage Foundation, Washington, D.C., April 19, 1994.

Books

Althoff, John and Stephen Babb, Editors. *Revolution in Central America.* Boulder, Colorado: Westview Press, 1983.

American Civil Liberties Union and Americas Watch Committee. *Report on Human Rights in El Salvador.* New York: Vintage Books, 1982.

Americas Watch. *El Salvador's Decade of Terror: Human Rights Since the Assassination of Archbishop Romero.* New York and London: Yale University Press, 1991.

Armstrong, Robert and Janet Shenk. *El Salvador: The Face of Revolution.* London, 1982.

Anderson, Thomas P. *Matanza: El Salvador's Communist Revolt of 1932.* Lincoln:University of Nebraska Press, 1971.

Anderson, Thomas P. *The War of the Dispossessed: Honduras and El Salvador, 1969.* Lincoln and London: University of Nebraska Press, 1981.

Arnson, Cynthia. *Crossroads: Congress, the Reagan Administration, and Central America.* New York: Pantheon Books, 1989.

Arnson, Cynthia. *El Salvador: A Revolution Confronts the United States.* Washington, D.C.: Institute for Policy Studies, 1982.

Baloyra, Enrique A. *El Salvador in Transition.* Chapel Hill and London: University of North Carolina Press, 1982.

Barry, Tom and Deb Preusch. *The Central America Fact Book.* New York: Grove Press, 1986.

Bermann, Karl. *Under the Big Stick: Nicaragua and the United States Since 1948.* Boston: South End Press, 1989.

Berryman, Phillip. *Inside Central America.* New York: Pantheon Books, 1985.

Berryman, Phillip. *The Religious Roots of Rebellion: Christians in Central America.* Maryknoll, N.Y.: Orbis, 1984.

Best, Edward. *US Policy and Regional Security in Central America.* Aldershot, England: Gower Publishing Company, 1987.

Binford, Leigh and Aldo Lauria-Santiago. *Landscapes of Struggle: Politics, Society and Community in El Salvador.* Pittsburgh: University of Pittsburgh Press, 2004.

Bibliography

Binford, Leigh. *The El Mozote Massacre.* Tucson: University of Arizona Press, 1996.

Blum, William. *Killing Hope: U.S. Military and CIA Interventions Since World War II.* Monroe, Maine: Common Courage Press, 2004.

Bonner, Raymond. *Weakness and Deceit: U.S. Policy and El Salvador.* New York: Times Books, 1984.

Bracamonte, Jose Angel Moroni and David E. Spencer. *Strategy and Tactics of the Salvadoran FMLN Guerrillas: Last Battle of the Cold War, Blueprint for Future Conflicts.* Westport, Connecticut: Praeger, 1995.

Brockett, Charles D. *Political Movements and Violence in Central America.* New York: Cambridge University Press, 2005.

Brockman, James R. *Oscar Romero, Bishop and Martyr.* New York: Orbis Books,   Maryknoll, 1982.

Brown, Jeremy M. *Explaining the Reagan Years in Central America: A World System Perspective.* New York and London: University Press of America, 1995.

Byrne, Hugh. *El Salvador's Civil War: A Study of Revolution.* Boulder and London: Lynne Rienner Publishers, 1996.

Brenda Carter, et.al. *A Dream Compels Us: Voices of Salvadoran Women.*

Boston: South End Press, 1989.

Child, Jack. *The Central American Peace Process, 1983-1991: Sheathing Swords, Building Confidence.* Boulder and London: Lynne Rienner Publishers, 1992.

Chomsky, Noam. *Deterring Democracy.* New York: Hill and Wang, 1992.

Chomsky, Noam. *On Power and Ideology: The Managua Lectures.* Boston: South End Press, 1987.

Chomsky, Noam. *Turning the Tide: U.S. Intervention in Central America and the Struggle for Peace.* Boston: South End Press, 1985.

Chomsky, Noam. *The New Military Humanism: Lessons From Kosovo.* Common Courage Press, 2002.

Christian, Shirley. *Nicaragua: Revolution in the Family.* New York: Vintage, 1986.

Charles Clements, *Witness to War: An American Doctor in El Salvador.* New York: Bantam, 1984.

Coatsworth, John H. *Central America and the United States: The Clients and the Colussus.* New York: Twayne Publishers, 1994.

Cockburn, Alexander. *Corruptions of Empire: Life Studies and the Reagan Era.* Haymarket Press, 1988.

El Salvador - A War by Proxy

Coleman, Kenneth M. and George C. Herring, Editors. *Understanding the Central America Crisis: Sources of Conflict, U.S. Policy and Options for Peace.* Wilmington, Delaware: Scholarly Resources, Inc., 1991.

Danner, Mark. *The Massacre at El Mozote.* New York: Vintage Books, 1993.

DePalma, Giuseppe and Laurence Whitehead. *The Central American Impasse.* London and Sydney: Croon Helm, 1986.

Didion, Joan. *Salvador.* New York: Pocket Books, 1983.

Duarte, Jose Napolean with Diana Page. *Duarte: My Story.* New York: G.P. Putnam's Sons, 1986.

Dunkerley, James. *The Long War: Dictatorship and Revolution in El Salvador.* London: Junction Books, 1982.

Farer, Tom J. and Ernest van den Haag.*U.S. Ends and Means in Central America: A Debate.* New York and London: Plenum Press, 1988.

Feinberg, Richard E., Editor. *Central America: International Dimensions of the Crisis.* New York and London: Holmes and Meier Publishers, Inc., 1982.

Fish, Joe and Christina Sganga. *El Salvador: Testament of Terror.* New York: Olive Branch Press, 1988.

Gaddis, John Paul. *Strategies of Containment: A Critical Appraisal of American National Security Policy During the Cold War.* Revised and Expanded Edition. Oxford and New York: Oxford University Press, 2005.

Galdamez, Pablo. *Faith of a People: The Life of a Basic Christian Community in El Salvador.* Maryknoll, N.Y.: Orbis, 1986.

Gatehouse, Mike and Mandy Macdonald. *In the Mountains of Morazan: Portrait of a Returned Refugee Community in El Salvador.* London: Central Books, 1995.

Gettleman, Marvin E, et.al., Editors. *El Salvador: Central America in the New Cold War.* New York: Grove Press, 1981.

Gerson, Allan. *The Kirkpatrick Mission: Diplomacy Without Apology.* New York: Free Press, 1991.

Gilly, Adolfo. *Guerra y politica en El Salvador.* Mexico: Editorial Nueva Imagen, 1981.

Gorkin, Michael and Gloria Leal, Marta Pineta. *From Grandmother to Granddaughter: Salvadoran Women's Stories.* Berkeley: University of California Press, 2000.

Grandin, Greg. *Empire's Workshop: Latin America, The United States, and the Rise of the New Imperialism.* New York: Metropolitan Books, 2006.

Grandin, Greg. *The Last Colonial Massacre: Latin America in the Cold War.*

Bibliography

Chicago and London: University of Chicago, 2004.

Grenier, Yvonne. *Guerre et Pouvoir au Salvador. Ideologies du Changement et Changement Ideologique.* Sante-Foy: Les Presses de L'Universite Laval, 1994.

Haas, Michael. *Cambodia, Pol Pot, and the United States: The Faustian Pact.* New York: Praeger, 1991.

Hahn, Walter F., Editor. *Central America and the Reagan Doctrine.* Lanham, Maryland: University Press of America, 1987.

Haig, Alexander. *Inner Circle: How America Changed the World.* Grand Central Publishing, 1994.

Herman, Edward S. and Frank Brodhead, *Demonstration Election: U.S.-Staged Elections in the Dominican Republic, Vietnam and El Salvador.* Boston: South End Press, 1984.

Hoppe, Hans Hermann. *Democracy: The God That Failed.* London: Transaction Publishers, 2001.

Johnstone, Ian. *Rights and Reconciliation: UN Strategies in El Salvador.* Boulder and London: Lynne Rienner Publishers, 1995.

Keogh, Dermit, Editor. *Central America: Human Rights and U.S. Foreign Policy.* Republic of Ireland: Cork University Press, 1985.

Keogh, Dermit. *Romero, El Salvador's Martyr.* Dublin, Ireland: Dominican Publications, 1981.

Lamperti, John W. *Enrique Alvarez Cordova: Life of Salvadoran Revolutionary and Gentleman.* Jefferson, North Carolina: McFarland and Company Publishers, 2006.

Landau, Saul. *The Guerrilla War of Central America: Nicaragua, El Salvador and Guatemala.* New York: St. Martin's Press, 1993.

Lafeber, Walter. *The New Empire: A Interpretation of American Expansion, 1860-*1898 (Ithaca, New York: Cornell University Press, 1963.

Leiken, Robert, Editor. *Central America: Anatomy of a Conflict.* New York: Pergamon, 1984.

Leiken, Robert. *Soviet Strategy in Latin America.* Washington, D.C.: Center for Strategic and International Studies, 1982.

LeoGrande, William M. Our Own Backyard: The United States in Central America, 1977-1992. Chapel Hill: University of North Carolina Press, 1998.

Leonard, Thomas M. *Central America and the United States: The Search for Stability* Athens: University of Georgia Press, 1991.

Lernoux, Penny. *Cry of the People.* New York: Doubleday, 1980.

Lindo-Fuentes, Hector and Erik Ching, Rafael A. Lara-Martinez.

Remembering a Massacre in El Salvador. Albuquerque: University of New Mexico Press, 2007.

Mahan, Alfred Thayer. *The Interest of America in Sea Power* (Boston: Little and Brown, 1897.

Martz, John D., Editor. *United States Policy in Latin America: A Quarter Century of Crisis and Challenge, 1961-1986.* Lincoln, Nebraska and London, England: University of Nebraska Press, 1988.

Martz, John D., Editor. *United States Policy in Latin America: A Decade of Crisis and Challenge, 1980-1990.* Lincoln, Nebraska: University of Nebraska Press, 1995.

May, Ernest R. *Imperial Democracy: The Emergence of America as a Great Power* (New York: Harcourt, Brace & World, 1961.

McClintock, Michael. *Instruments of Statecraft: U.S. Guerilla Warfare, Counterinsurgency, and Counterterrorism, 1940-1990.*Pantheon Books, Random House, 1992. Archived at http://www.statecraft.org/about.html.

McClintock, Michael. *The American Connection: State Terror and Popular Resistance in El Salvador.* London: Zed Books, 1985.

Means, Russell. *Where White Men Fear to Tread.* New York: St. Martin's Griffin, 1995.

McGuire, Peter H. *Facing Death in Cambodia.* New York: Columbia University Press, 2005.

Menjivar, Cecilia and Nestor Rodriguez, Editors. *When States Kill: Latin America, the U.S., and Technologies of Terror.* Austin, Texas: University of Texas Press, 2005.

Middlebrook, Kevin J. and Carlos Rico, Editors. *The United States and Latin America in the 1980s: Contending Perspectives on a Decade of Crisis.* Pittsburgh: University of Pittsburgh Press, 1986.

Montgomery, Tommie Sue. *Revolution in El Salvador: Origins and Evolution.* Boulder, Colorado: Westview Press, 1982.

Montgomery, Tommie Sue. *Revolution in El Salvador: From Civil Strife to Civil Peace.* Boulder, Colorado: Westview Press, 1995.

Moreno, Dario. *U. S. Policy in Central America: The Endless Debate.* Miami: Florida University Press, 1990.

Morris, James A. and Steve C. Ropp, Editors. *Central America: Crisis and Adaption.* Albuquerque: University of New Mexico Press, 1984.

Murray, Kevin. *El Salvador: Peace on Trial.* Oxfam UK and Ireland, 1997.

Nelson-Pallmeyer, Jack. *War Against the Poor: Low-Intensity Conflict and*

Bibliography

Christian Faith. Maryknoll, New York: Orbis Books, 1989.

North, Liisa. *Bitter Grounds: Roots of Revolt in El Salvador*. Toronto, 1981.

Parenti, Michael. *The Sword and the Dollar: Imperialism, Revolution and the Arms Race*. St. Martin's Press, 1988.

Pastor, Robert. *Condemned to Repetition: The United States and Nicaragua*. Princeton University Press, 1987.

Jenny Pearce. *Promised Land: Peasant Rebellion in Chalatenango, El Salvador*. London: Latin American Bureau, 1986.

Pearce, Jenny. *Under the Eagle*. London, 1982.

Prothero, Mitchell. "Hezbollah Strengthens Its Grip in Lebanon," *U. S. News & World Report*, August 4, 2008.

Rouquie. Alan. *The Military and the State in Latin America*, trans. Paul E. Sigmund. Berkeley: University of California Press, 1987.

Rosenberg, Tina. *Children of Cain: Violence and the Violent in Latin America*. New York: William Morrow and Company, 1991.

Russell, Philip. *El Salvador in Crisis*. Colorado River Press, 1984.

Ruwart, Mary. *Healing Our World*. Kalamazoo, Michigan: Sun Star Press, 1992.

Schoultz, Lar. *Beneath the United States: A History of U.S. Policy Towards Latin America*. Cambridge and London: Harvard University Press, 1998.

Scott, Peter Dale and Jonathan Marshall. *Cocaine Politics: Drugs, Armies and the CIA in Central America*. University of California Press, 1991.

Short, Philip. *Pol Pot: Anatomy of a Nightmare*. Henry Colt and Company, 2005.

Shultz, George P. *Turmoil and Triumph: My Years as Secretary of State*. New York: Charles Scribner's Sons, 1993.

Sikkink, Kathryn. *Mixed Signals: U.S. Human Rights Policy and Latin America*. Ithaca: Cornell University Press, 2004.

Smith, Bruce L. R., Editor. *The Next Steps in Central America*. Washington, D.C.: Brookings Institution, 1991.

Smith, Christian. *Resisting Reagan: The U.S. Central America Peace Movement*. Chicago and London: University of Chicago Press, 1996.

Smith, Gaddis. *Morality, Reason and Power: American Diplomacy in the Carter Years*. (New York, Hill and Wang, 1986).

Sneh, Itai Nartzizenfield. *The Future Almost Arrived: How Jimmy Carter Failed to Change U.S. Foreign Policy*. New York: Peter Lang Publishing, 2008.

Steel, Ronald. *Walter Lippman and the American Century*. Boston: Little and Brown, 1980.

El Salvador - A War by Proxy

Towell, Larry. *El Salvador*. New York and London: W.W. Norton, 1997.

Ucles, Mario Lungo. *El Salvador in the Eighties: Counterinsurgency and Revolution*. Philadelphia: Temple University Press, 1996.

Vigil, Jose Ignacio Lopez. *Rebel Radio: The Story of El Salvador's Radio Venceremos*. Willimantic, Connecticut: Curbstone Press, 1991.

Walker, William. *The War in Nicaragua*. Mobile, Alabama: S. H. Goetzel, 1860.

Walter, Knut and Philip J. Williams. *Militarization and Demilitarization in El Salvador's Transition to Democracy*. Pittsburgh: University of Pittsburgh Press, 1997.

Webre, Stephen. *Jose Napolean Duarte and the Christian Democratic Party in Salvadoran Politics, 1960-1972*. Louisiana State University Press, Baton Rouge, La., 1979.

Wesson, Robert. *U.S. Influence in Latin America in the 1980s*. Stanford, California: Hoover Institution Press, 1982.

Wheaton, Philip. *Agrarian Reform in El Salvador*. Washington, D.C.: Ecumenical Program for Interamerican Communication and Action, p. 1980.

White, Robert Alan. *The Morass: United States Intervention in Central America*. New York: Harper and Row Publishers, 1984.

Whitfield, Teresa. *Paying the Price: Ignacio Ellacuria and the Murdered Jesuits of El Salvador*. Philadelphia: Temple University Press, 1995.

Wiarda, Howard J. *American Foreign Policy Toward Latin America in the 80s and 90s: Issues and Controversies from Reagan to Bush*. New York and London: New York University Press, 1992.

William Appleman Williams, *The Roots of the Modern American Empire* (New York: Random House, 1969.

Woodward, Bob. *VEIL: The Secret Wars of the CIA 1981-1987*. New York, 1987.

Wright, Jim. *Worth It All: My War for Peace*. Washington and New York: Brassey's Books, 1993.

Zinn, Howard. *Declarations of Independence: Cross-Examining American Ideology*. Perennial Publishers, 1991.

Dissertations and Theses

Kruse, David Samuel Owens, "The Mass Media and United States Foreign Policy: The Case of El Salvador and the Land Question", Boston College, 1996.

Riedel, Curtis B., "The Long Search for Democratic Stability in El Salvador: Implications for United States Policy", Naval Postgraduate School, Monterey,

Bibliography

California, Department of National Security Affairs, March, 1997.

Internet Sources

Jaffe, Maggie, "The Camera is a Shield": John Hoagland, Combat Photographer. Archived at http://thedagger.com/archive/elsal/.

Katsiavriades, Kryss and Talaat Qureshi, "Victims of US Foreign Policy". Archived at http://www.krysstal.com/democracy_whyusa06.html.

Pinter, Harold, "Innocent People Suffer", Lecture to the Swedish Academy at Stockholm, December 7, 2005. Archived at http://www.thewe.cc/contents/more/archive2006/torture_death_and_nicaragua.htm.

Third World Traveler, "1985 Censored Foreign Policy News Stories". Archived at http://www.thirdworldtraveler.com/Project%20Censored/CensoredNews_1985.html.

Van Auken, Bill, "Jeane Kirkpatrick: From "Social Democrat" to Champion of Death Squads", *World Socialist Web Site*, December 12, 2006.

Virtual Truth Commission, "Reports by Country: El Salvador". Archived at http://www.geocities.com/~virtualtruth/salvador.htm.

Publications

School of the Americas Watch

Research Papers

Benning, Bob, "War in El Salvador; The Policies of President Reagan and The Lessons Learned for Today", Arizona State University, April 15, 2003.

Speeches

White, Robert E. "Weakness, Deceit and Consequences", speech delivered at the University of Texas, April 17, 2008. Archived at http://www.ciponline.org/central_america/WhiteSpeechApril08.doc.

About the Author

Troy Keith Preston was born on October 29, 1966 in Lynchburg, Virginia, USA and currently resides in Richmond, Virginia, USA. He attended Timberlake Christian School in Lynchburg, Virginia and Jefferson Forest High School in Bedford County, Virginia.

He received his BA from the College of Humanities and Sciences' School of World Studies department at Virginia Commonwealth University in 2006. He previously attended Central Virginia Community College in Lynchburg, Virginia. As an independent journalist, he has been published by LewRockwell.Com, Anti-State.Com and AntiWar.Com. He was the winner of the 2008 Chris R. Tame Memorial Prize essay contest sponsored by the Libertarian Alliance in London, England. He completed his course work for an MA in History from Virginia Commonwealth University in May 2009, and passed his master's thesis defense with distinction on April 29, 2009.

9 781908 476319